THE KLINEFELTER LEGACY

A STORY OF FAITH, FAMILY AND FORGIVENESS

"*The Klinefelter Legacy* exposes raw emotion, straight-up questions, and religious conviction. With brutal honesty, the author exposes the criminal actions that left two young men lying dead on frozen highways. 'What a waste,' several observed about that night. But faith and forgiveness will warm the reader's heart."

—Pastor Steve Schoepf, Westwood Community Church, St. Cloud

"My wife, Kelly, and I also lost our son, Saint Paul Police Officer Ron Ryan Jr, [who was] killed in the line of duty. His also was a very senseless murder that occurred seventeen months before Brian lost his life. We met the remarkable Klinefelter family the night of Brian's wake. We have stayed in touch through the years, as we shared stories of how our families have evolved since we faced these terrible events in our lives.

"This book is not just a positive legacy for Brian but a wonderful testimonial to all the Klinefelter family members. God bless them all!"

—Cdr. Ron Ryan, (Ret.) St. Paul Police Department

THE KLINEFELTER LEGACY

A STORY OF FAITH, FAMILY AND FORGIVENESS

By
Andy Marso

NORTH STAR PRESS OF ST. CLOUD, INC.
St. Cloud, Minnesota

ISBN: 978-1-68201-016-7

Printed in the United States of America.

First edition: January 2016

Published by:
North Star Press of St. Cloud, Inc.
P.O. Box 451
St. Cloud, MN 56302

northstarpress.com

Dedicated to Brian Klinefelter
and law enforcement officers everywhere
who serve their communities with honor.

Table of Contents

Preface

OUG THOMSEN maneuvered his Buick SUV down a straight, slim stretch of country road between St. Cloud and St. Stephen, retracing a path he took almost twenty years earlier with a gun to his head.

Thomsen could not remember the exact spot where the man had told him to pull the car over on the very narrow shoulder . . . where the man had told him to remove the three 100-pound bags of salt from the trunk of his rear-wheel-drive Ford Thunderbird and crawl into it . . . where Thomsen's fears had changed from the gun in the man's hand to the possibility that the man would wreck the car sliding on ice and kill them both or abandon it on some deserted road with Doug in the trunk, shivering, until hypothermia claimed him.

"It must have been right around here," Thomsen said.

There was nothing in Thomsen's background that would have foreshadowed that night in the trunk.

He had spent the previous two decades building a steady, low-profile life as a barber, cutting hair for eight or nine hours a day, five days a week. He'd married his high school sweetheart, bought a small house in a quiet city and had two kids, a son and a daughter.

On a typical day he worked at the barbershop, went home to dinner with his family and then went to one of the kids' many sporting events. He would mow the grass or shovel snow, depending on the season, help his elderly neighbors and go to church on Sundays. It was routine. It was comfortable. Thomsen was happy. His only contact with law enforcement was a few friends who worked in the industry and the cops who came into his shop for a trim.

And then one frigid January night a desperate, wild-eyed stranger with a gun came to Doug Thomsen's door.

By the end of that night two people were dead, two others were heading to prison, and dozens of lives were thrown into turmoil.

Thomsen and the others involved were left trying to make sense of the senselessness of the whole thing.

In the twenty years since, they have carved their own meanings into the icy events, turning the tragedies of that January night into triumphs of the human spirit by leaning on their families and their faith.

One family in particular would show the way.

Chapter One

Ruth Tamm, 1996

RUTH TAMM turned off the vacuum cleaner. All was quiet at Freeway Liquor, a small store at the top of a hill in central Minnesota, visible from Interstate 94. She unplugged the vacuum and started winding up the cord. Her shift had started at 5:00 p.m., and it had been a dull night.

New Year's 1996 had been less than a month ago. The Dallas Cowboys had defeated the Pittsburgh Steelers the night before in Super Bowl XXX, the month's other big liquor sales event. Hardly anyone came in to buy alcohol the day after the Super Bowl.

Tamm spent her days working in the administrative office at Albany High School making copies for teachers, working on the school newsletter and joking around with students waiting to talk to the principal. Her own kids had gone through the school and most of the students knew her.

At age forty-seven, she had taken a second job at the liquor store to occupy her evenings because her husband worked nights and her daughter had gone off to college. In Albany, a town of about 1,500 with the motto "Where Friendly Paths Cross," clerking at the liquor store often meant she could catch up on her reading and get paid to do it, especially on the Monday night after the Super Bowl.

In three-and-a half hours she had made three sales and helped one customer who came in to use the tanning beds in the back. Now the store was empty. It was just Tamm, waiting to close and go home.

She put the vacuum away, sat down by the store's front window and lit a cigarette. She adjusted her wire-rim glasses and ran her hand through her close-cropped brown hair.

Tamm blew a cloud of smoke on the window. Outside everything was dark and still—no movement at the café next door or the trailer park across the street. It was bitterly cold. Cold even for Minnesota in January. Every living thing, human or animal, seemed to be hunkered down. A blanket of snow on the ground further muffled the noise outside.

A pair of headlights appeared down the road, growing larger as they approached the store. A white pickup truck turned in. As it passed through the parking lot, Tamm could vaguely make out the faces of three youngish men inside.

She heard one of them yell, "Wa-hoo," as the truck skidded around a light post surrounded by a substantial snow bank.

Tamm shook her head. Must be kids from school who recognized her car and thought she might sell them alcohol.

"What are these kids doing out on such a cold night?" she muttered to herself.

The truck pulled around to the rear of the building, temporarily out of sight. Tamm waited a few moments, blowing one last puff of smoke, then extinguishing her cigarette.

Three figures emerged from around the side of the building on foot. They wore ski masks, two royal blue and one black. Their breath puffed out in clouds of steam from the mouth holes of the masks.

Tamm got up and walked around the counter to the glass door at the front of the store. She had locked it earlier when she was in the back stocking shelves, and now she flicked the deadbolt to the unlocked position and held the door open to let the trio in.

"Kind of chilly out there tonight, huh?" she said.

They didn't answer. Instead, the three men walked past her and went toward the beer coolers in the rear.

The store was small, no more than twenty feet wide from the counter next to the front door to the unisex restroom on the opposite wall. It ran maybe twice that in length, from the front door to the beer coolers.

The men left their masks on, but that wasn't odd to her. They'd just come in from the frigid air and sometimes in the winter kids wore ski masks in the store when trying to buy underage. She prepared herself to card these three.

One grabbed a couple cases of beer, cradling them under his arms. Another, who she noticed was wearing latex surgical gloves, eyed a row of liquor bottles. Above him hung a large fish mounted on the wood paneling that ran the length of the room above the shelves. Two of the men stopped short of the counter, but the third kept coming toward her.

"Open the till and give me the money," he growled.

Tamm stared at him, not speaking. *Is this some kind of joke?* she wondered.

"Open the till," the man said again, more forcefully.

"What?" she said. She studied the speaker, trying to figure out from the exposed skin around his eyes and mouth which kid from the high school he could be.

"Don't case me over," the man growled. "Don't case me over."

He reached into his pants and pulled out something small and black. "Open the fuckin' till or I'll shoot you," he said, jabbing the object in her direction.

Tamm stood, mute, searching her memory for who that voice might belong to.

Her dad and her brother had long guns they used for hunting, but handguns were foreign to her. In her head she had an image of them being silver or metallic. This black one looked more like something her kids would play with.

She still thought the man in front of her was probably a kid from school, but if this was a joke, it had stopped being funny. She stared at him blankly, a warm, dizzying feeling somewhere between fear and anger creeping up from her chest to her head.

"Don't screw with me," the man yelled, shaking the gun at her. "Open the till."

Tamm finally made herself move, but her hands were shaking, and her mind was unable to conjure up the sequence of buttons she needed to push to open the cash register without making a sale.

She fumbled along as the man in the mask kept the gun trained on her.

His friend with the rubber gloves took a few steps forward and glanced toward the front door. "C'mon, hurry up," he said, his voice cracking. "This is taking too long."

"Haven't you ever been held up before?" the gunman shouted at her.

"No, no, I'm new at this," Tamm stammered. She tried to laugh to diffuse the tension, but her voice caught in her throat. Her quivering fingers mashed the register keys.

"This is taking too long!" the man with the rubber gloves said again.

"Open the fuckin' till," the gunman yelled.

"I don't know how!" Tamm screamed back.

The register suddenly sprang open. Tamm grabbed a paper bag from beneath the counter and started shoveling the contents of the cash register into it.

The man with the gun peered over the counter, watching the transfer.

"I don't want the checks," he said, gesturing with the gun. "Just the cash."

Tamm reached for the rolls of quarters at one end of the register.

"Just the bills," the gunman clarified.

Tamm's breathing began to slow as she filled the bag. She could do this. These men would take what they wanted and then leave. She would be okay.

When the bills were out of the register she handed the bag over to the gunman.

The man with the rubber gloves had moved right up by the register, his eyes still on the front door. "This is taking too long," he hissed one more time.

The man with the gun looked at him quickly, then back at Tamm.

"Where's the bathroom?" he asked her.

"Right over there," she said, pointing behind him at the opposite wall. The bathroom was no more than six feet away, just inside the front door on the right.

The gunman looked in that direction. He hesitated, the arm holding the gun dropping a little. He turned back to Tamm.

"Well, go in the back room," he ordered her, pointing the gun again. He reached his other hand into his pocket and pulled out a length of rope.

Tamm's heart started thumping. She just wanted them to leave. If they tied her up in the back no one was likely to find her until the next day.

"No," she said.

"Whaddya mean, no?" The gunman said, his eyes growing wide behind the ski mask and his voice rising. "Get in the back room!"

"What are you gonna do with me?" she asked. "You don't need to tie me up."

"Just get in the back room," the gunman said, glancing back at his companions, who were fidgeting and glancing around nervously.

She needed to buy some time to think. What if she were to try to run? She realized she was in her stocking feet.

"I need to put on my shoes," she said.

The man with the gun grunted, but gestured for her to do so. "Hurry up, then," he said.

Tamm put one foot in her shoe and weighed her options as she began to lace it up. There was little she could do. She didn't think she could outrun these young guys and even if she did, where could she go? Out into the snow and cold? If she was lucky a car might pass by, but she hadn't seen enough traffic that evening to have any confidence that would happen.

By the time she finished lacing the other shoe, Tamm was resigned to doing as she was told.

"All right now, hurry up and get in the back room," the gunman said.

She started walking toward the back of the store, and the three men followed her.

They headed into the stockroom, past concrete walls lined with kegs, excess twenty-four-packs of beer and a few boxes that held bottles of cheap hard liquor. A walk-in refrigerator stood against one wall. She felt the man with the gun grip her shoulder and turn her toward it.

"Go in the cooler," he said, beckoning toward it with the gun.

The guy with the rubber gloves walked over and opened the door, holding it and looking at her through his ski mask. An icy cloud wafted out of the open door.

"I'm not going in the cooler," Tamm said. "I'll freeze to death in there. You put me in there, I can't get out. My husband isn't home, and nobody will find me 'til morning."

"C'mon man," the guy holding the case of beer said to the gunman. "We gotta go."

The gunman's grip on her shoulder tightened. She could almost feel his frustration.

"Get on the floor, then," he said.

"No, I'll just sit on these beer cases," Tamm said, gesturing to a pile of twenty-four-packs.

"Fine, just sit down," the gunman said.

"What are you going to do?" Tamm asked.

"Tie you up so you can't get loose," the gunman said.

She sat down on the crates of beer, facing him. The man handed the gun off to his friend, who held it at his side while continuing to cradle the two cases of beer under his other arm. The third man, with the rubber gloves, had disappeared.

The one who had first held the gun grabbed Tamm's arms, pulled her hands behind her back and swiftly tied them.

"I won't get out of here 'til morning," she said.

The gunman looked back. The man with the rubber gloves had returned, his arms now stacked with beer and a bottle of rum.

The gunman turned back to Tamm.

"We use this all the time. This is washline rope," he said. "It stretches really easy."

He reached behind her back again and pulled her hands away from each other, showing her how elastic the restraints were.

"Once we're gone, you can get out of there real easy," he said. "It won't take you long."

Tamm watched as the three of them left out the back, through the exterior stockroom door.

So that's why they parked back there.

She could hear the truck rev up and the sound of heavy tires crunching in the snow.

Once she was sure they were gone, Tamm stood and made her way back to the cash register, her hands still tied behind her back. The store was deserted. She backed up to the front wall and crouched low, feeling around blindly until she found the small red button she was supposed to press in the event of a robbery.

Then she went to work freeing her hands. The man had been right—the laundry line stretched, and she was able to wriggle out of it a little at a time. Within minutes, Tamm was loose. She grabbed the store's phone from the front counter and punched 911, setting in motion a law enforcement response that would span several agencies.

Chapter Two

Ruth Tamm,
Nineteen Years Later

THE FULL WEIGHT of what happened to Ruth Tamm that night—and what could have happened—did not hit her until days later when she watched a funeral on television.

When the police arrived at the liquor store, she was still convinced the three men had targeted the store because they knew her or one of her kids.

"I'm surprised I'm alive, now that I look back on it," Tamm said nineteen years later, sitting in the café that shared the parking lot with that same liquor store. "But I was so sure it was some kids from school. I even told the cops I was so sure it was somebody from the school that, the next day, they'd see me and laugh their asses off that they got to pull this over on me. I was determined to go to school and drive around until I saw that white pickup."

Tamm laughed, but then quickly turned serious. Since that night she has wondered whether there was anything she could have done to make things end differently.

What if she had left the door locked? What if she had taken the trio more seriously when she was up front, emptying the cash register with the gun trained on her?

"Had I hit the panic button when I was standing there, when this was going on, it could have probably been a whole different story," she said.

Moments later she acknowledged that might not be true. Albany had only one police officer on duty at a time, and the response to the silent alarm might not have been immediate. Pressing the button might have only gotten her killed.

Still, she wondered. And she watched the funeral with a mix of fear and sadness.

"It was very sad to think I was the whole cause of all this," Tamm said. "Felt bad for this family that had lost their husband and dad, but I had to do what I had to do. I didn't really expect them to get caught. Robberies happen all the time, and nobody catches them."

Tamm pushed up her black-framed glasses, which had gotten thicker since she was robbed, and wiped a tear before it could fall down her cheek. She changed the subject.

Soon after the robbery, she learned the three men were not from Albany High School. They weren't from Albany at all. They didn't know her. They had chosen Albany because one of them did some day labor there for a farmer once and knew it was a sleepy town on the freeway. They chose the liquor store only after learning that the Kentucky Fried Chicken they planned to rob had already closed for the night.

It was an event that was hard to make sense of. She'd taken the liquor store job to stay busy—danger hadn't crossed her mind.

"That stuff just doesn't happen around here," Tamm said.

And then it did. Then it happened to *her*, and she didn't know why she survived that night when others didn't. She hadn't exactly been cooperative with the robbers, but maybe that saved her.

"I was stupid," Tamm said. "'Course, they probably thought I was like their mom, and that's why I'm still here to talk about it."

The robbery changed things for a while.

Her nephew spent the night at her house for a few weeks so she wouldn't have to be alone while her husband was at work.

She returned to the liquor store and worked a few more shifts before deciding she couldn't do it anymore.

But instead of withdrawing, Tamm reached out.

She spoke about the robbery to several classes at the high school, some of which included students who also worked nights at fast food places or convenience stores. She told them what she could to prepare them for the possibility of looking up and seeing a gun pointed at them, even in their small town.

Tamm still wanted to work a second job but decided there was something more she was supposed to be doing with her time. "I figured I should start looking after old people instead of liquor stores," Tamm said.

She and her sister started a home care business. They collected a handful of clients, for whom they cooked, cleaned, did laundry and whatever else the elderly clients needed to remain in their homes.

"I love it," Tamm said.

She had very little contact with law enforcement before that night and she's had very little since, with one exception. Her niece became an officer with the Minneapolis Police Department. Tamm said they have not spoken about that night.

"I always tell her, 'Be careful,' though," Tamm said.

Chapter Three

Brian Klinefelter, 1996

THE WHITE PICKUP truck skidded out of the liquor store parking lot and headed toward Interstate 94, exhaust billowing from the tailpipe into the Arctic air.

Inside, three men removed their ski masks and gave adrenaline-fueled shouts after successfully completing a heist more serious than any of the petty crimes that checkered their backgrounds before that night.

Thomas Leo Kantor, twenty-six, was behind the wheel. The baby-faced Kantor's usually sleepy eyes were wide with excitement. His past included convictions for stealing guns, hot-wiring cars and passing bad checks. He was on probation. He had stolen the white pickup. Now he had also held a gun on a liquor store clerk while robbing her.

In the passenger seat sat Brian Scott Ederhoff, also twenty-six, who had attended Sartell High School with Kantor. Neither had finished school. Kantor had married Ederhoff's sister years earlier, but they had since separated.

Ederhoff had an angular face and wore big eyeglasses below a large forehead made even larger by receding hair that in the back hung down past his shoulders. He'd had his driver's license suspended three times for speeding, driving without insurance, and other infractions. Police had picked up Ederhoff the previous winter after he got drunk and passed out in a snowdrift.

Between the two of them sat Kenneth Michael Roering, who was just nineteen. Roering had met the other two through a mutual friend. He had thick eyebrows, a dark mustache and goatee, and ears that jutted out from his head. He had just gotten out of jail after serving thirty days for selling pot to an undercover cop. His record also included speeding tickets, a minor-in-possession-of-alcohol citation, and a pending court date for violating a restraining order.

As Kantor maneuvered the truck onto the freeway, the other two set about divvying up the money from the robbery. It amounted to $372 dollars, total.

Roering and Ederhoff would later say that the robbery was Kantor's idea, and they were just going along with it. At the time the two didn't know that Kantor, who was adopted, had told his biological mother that he had a premonition that when he died there would be lights and sirens and gunfire. And he was not afraid of that death.

* * *

ST. JOSEPH POLICE OFFICER Brian Klinefelter was supposed to leave work early that night. He had some time off coming to him and a daughter only a few months old waiting at home. Chief Brad Lindgren had told him he could head back to his family a few hours before his shift officially ended that night.

But a call about a robbery in Albany came over the radio, so Klinefelter stayed in his squad car on Highway 75. If the perpetrators were heading for St. Cloud, they might exit I-94 and take 75 into the city, he figured.

At age twenty-five, Klinefelter had everything he wanted. He had started on the force three years earlier, after dreaming about being cop since childhood. One year after taking the job, he married his high school sweetheart, Wendy, and a year later they had Katelyn, who was not part of the plan but a very happy accident.

Klinefelter was a big man, six-foot-four and 240 pounds, but those who knew him described him as gentle and affable. He lived a life common in central Minnesota, playing softball in the summer, riding snowmobiles in the winter and hunting in the fall. He and Wendy were planning to build a house soon and put down roots in a community that was quickly feeling like home.

St. Joseph, Minnesota, population 4,100, had a six-person police force, and Klinefelter reveled in the life of a small-town cop.

While on the beat, he would pop into the St. Joseph Meat Market to snag a piece of beef jerky or gab with cooks at Gary's Pizza, who let him make his own pie in the back.

But he was not afraid of the tough side of cop work. Lindgren had nominated him for a statewide award after Klinefelter coaxed a suicidal man with a shotgun out of his home following an hour-long standoff.

When Klinefelter heard the call that night over the radio, the dispatcher said three white males had robbed a female clerk at gunpoint at the Freeway Liquor Store in Albany. The clerk believed they were driving a white pickup truck. Obviously, she knew they were armed.

Within fifteen minutes of the call, Klinefelter saw a white pickup go by, heading east toward St. Cloud. He could see three heads in the cab of the truck. He let it pass him, and then pulled onto the road behind it.

Klinefelter peered forward into the darkness, trying to get a look at the license plate, but it was covered in snow.

He punched the dispatch button on his radio and called it in.

"Did she say it was an older vehicle?" he asked. "I'm following a white Chevy pickup truck, newer model, three occupants, eastbound on 75. I'll be stopping them on County Road 133."

The dispatcher said, "10-4,"then asked other cars in the area to provide backup.

Klinefelter flipped on his lights and sirens. Within moments the truck up ahead was slowing down and pulling onto the shoulder.

They were on the east edge of St. Joseph, past the town's lone stoplight on the corner with the gas station and diner. It was a four-lane highway divided by a grassy median in sparsely wooded prairie, dotted with a few commercial buildings which were dark and empty at that hour.

Klinefelter got out of the squad car and approached the driver's side of the pickup truck, his left hand shining his flashlight and his right hand resting on his holstered sidearm.

On the other side of the median, seventeen-year-old Tiffany Breth was westbound on Highway 75 in a gray Chevy Nova.

Breth lived in Opole, northwest of St. Cloud. She had driven into the city after school for her job at JC Penney and, her shift over, was on her way to her boyfriend's house.

On that very cold night, the highway seemed a little slick so Breth was driving slowly. As she came into St. Joseph, she saw the flashing lights of a police car parked along the road on the other side of the median. She slowed down even more and craned her neck to see what was going on.

A large police officer stood by the driver's door of a pickup truck, a white Chevy full-size. He was shining his flashlight into the cab of the truck.

Breth was almost parallel to the truck when she saw an arm reach out from inside it. A loud crack rent the still night, and she saw the officer fall backward, his arms spreading wide and his head snapping violently onto the pavement.

She gasped.

The white truck's tires spun on the icy shoulder, then caught, and the vehicle sped away.

Breth didn't know what happened. Her first thought was that the officer might have had a heart attack or stroke, as quickly as he collapsed. But the people in the truck were leaving, and there was no one else there to call 911.

In an instant, Breth made a decision to help. She punched the accelerator and the car lurched forward. At a break in the median up ahead, she cranked the steering wheel and made a U-turn, pulling up past the police car, which was still parked with its lights flashing.

Breth maneuvered her little car so it was diagonal in the road, shielding the officer's body. She put the Nova in park, punched her hazard lights and jumped out, leaving the car running and the driver's side door open as she rushed to the fallen man's side.

The officer's flashlight lay on the ground ten or twelve feet away, and she thought maybe the person in the truck had grabbed it and hit him in the head with it.

She picked it up and shined it on the officer. Blood was spreading over the payment around his head and neck. Breth knelt down next to him and shook his shoulder.

"Can you hear me?" she yelled. "What happened? Can you hear me?"

No response.

Blood bubbled around the officer's mouth, causing steam to rise in the frigid night air.

Breth ran up the road, frantically looking for a car she could flag down for help. There was no one.

She ran back to the officer on the ground and knelt down beside him again.

"You're gonna be okay," she said, tears forming in her eyes. "Hang on. Help is coming."

Soon another police car emerged from the darkness, its lights flashing, and parked behind her car.

An officer climbed out of the driver's side and jogged toward her, his hand on his holstered gun.

"What happened?" the officer yelled.

"I don't know," Breth said. "I don't know. There was this white truck, and it just drove off."

The man knelt beside the fallen officer on the ground in a pool of now-frozen blood.

"We need an ambulance," he said.

The officer gripped his shoulder radio and spoke into it.

Breth heard him say the words "possible gunshot wound," and they cut through her fog of fear.

All at once the pieces came together in her head. The noise. The fall. The blood.

She'd watched the officer on the ground get shot.

Chapter Four

Nineteen Years Later

BRIAN KLINEFELTER'S law enforcement legacy was secure by the time he fell to the pavement that January night. Twenty years later, it lives on in those he served.

Few owe Klinefelter more than Troy Koopmeiners, a forty-eight-year-old man who still lives in St. Joseph.

Three months before he was shot, Klinefelter responded to a call from a fellow officer requesting backup to deal with a domestic disturbance.

Koopmeiners, then twenty-eight, had assaulted his wife at her parents' house, then fled to his own house, where he called her and said he was either going to shoot himself or burn the house down.

Koopmeiners was known to the small St. Joseph Police Department and had been confrontational with officers in the past.

Brian Klinefelter was among those who had arrested Koopmeiners before. When he arrived at the scene that day, he used a cell phone to call Koopmeiners, who was still holed up inside the house.

Chief Lindgren arrived soon after, but the job of talking Koopmeiners down had by then already fallen to Klinefelter.

"This guy was really despondent and he had a loaded gun," Lindgren recalled twenty years later. "He was ready to take himself out or take us out."

Lindgren said Koopmeiners never specifically threatened the officers' lives, but during an hour-long conversation with Klinefelter, he told them repeatedly not to come in, and he threatened suicide multiple times.

He said he did not want to go to jail again.

Klinefelter did his best to calm Koopmeiners as Lindgren and another officer on the scene went door-to-door at nearby houses, clearing out anyone within firing range.

At one point, Koopmeiners hung up on Klinefelter. But Klinefelter reestablished contact and again tried to talk Koopmeiners into surrendering peacefully.

Eventually he wore him down. Koopmeiners came out of the house unarmed, with his hands in the air, and was taken into custody without incident.

When officers entered the house they found a pump-action shotgun, loaded, with a round chambered and the safety off, sitting by the phone.

Koopmeiners was charged with a gross misdemeanor assault, but the day appeared to mark a turning point in his life. He had one more DWI in June of 1996, but in the nineteen years that followed his record shows only minor traffic violations.

For the cool Klinefelter showed under pressure, Lindgren nominated his young officer for the Minnesota Chiefs of Police Association's Distinguished Service Medal, commonly known as the Officer of the Year Award.

Lindgren wanted Klinefelter's gregarious, engaging manner to be a model for other officers.

"The most important weapon you have is your ability to defuse situations, speak with people, engage," Lindgren said. "That's your best weapon and your first weapon."

Klinefelter deployed that weapon countless times in his short career.

The night Klinefelter was shot, St. Joseph resident Mary Christen Czech was settling down to read in bed, burrowing in against the chill, when she heard what she thought was a car backfiring. Then the air was filled with sirens.

Czech's son Nigel had Asperger's syndrome, a form of high-functioning autism marked by difficulty navigating social situations, but no one knew that until he was thirty. Growing up, he was thought to be a difficult child, one who frustrated teachers, coaches, and his parents with his inability to read their emotions.

"When other people would get mad at him, instead of backing off, he would keep going forward," Czech said. "It seemed like he was trying to get in your face, and it was just that he didn't understand that people who are angry with him have a certain tone and it's best not to push. That's one of the cues that he didn't get."

One night twenty years ago, seventeen-year-old Nigel was challenging Czech and her husband, getting in their faces, and they felt out of options.

"We thought, just to calm things down, we should have police come and separate him," she said.

Brian Klinefelter and another St. Joseph officer showed up at her door that night.

She remembered being struck by how the towering Klinefelter calmly approached her son and said, "Hey, buddy, let's you and I go talk." His tone, she said, was more like an older brother than "the law."

Klinefelter and Nigel disappeared into Nigel's bedroom while the other officer talked to Czech and her husband. A few minutes later, Klinefelter emerged, and the situation had been defused. Nigel was calm.

"When they left, Officer Klinefelter said, 'Here's my number. Give me a call if you just want to chat, and he can call me any time if he wants to go shoot hoops or something,'" Czech remembered.

A few days later, the phone rang at her house. It was Klinefelter, just calling to check in.

A few days after that phone call, he was shot on the road less than two blocks from their house.

When she told Nigel about it the next day, he just kept shaking his head.

"We just saw him," she remembered Nigel saying, over and over.

Czech said she's heard stories about police officers who were confrontational, who lost their tempers and escalated situations. She knew things could have gone differently the night she and her husband called for help with Nigel.

"Here came this tall police officer who could have also been kind of commanding and in your face, but he was just very kind and very gentle, very friendly, not putting Nigel down, not patronizing," Czech said.

She says that, when her son found out he had Asperger's thirteen years later, he looked into it online and found that several famous and successful people also had Asperger's. His diagnosis came as a relief, an explanation for his differences.

He got a job in the Twin Cities, working in quality control, a field in which his meticulous attention to detail was highly valued. His relationship with his mother remained strong and he was successful.

Czech said the family owed some of that success to a small-town police officer who took an interest in her son.

"Brian Klinefelter exemplified the best of that profession," Czech said.

Told the story almost twenty years later, Lindgren said he did not know about it, but he did not seem surprised.

"He would do the follow-up," Lindgren said. "A lot of police officers wouldn't. When you're taking thousands of calls a year, to go back and check up on somebody . . . that is rare, even in that day and age. And that was before community policing and all that other stuff came around."

Klinefelter did not have any training manuals about community policing, but he had his father, Dave.

"I always would get on Brian's case," Dave Klinefelter said. "I'd tell him, 'Now, Brian, make sure you're a community police officer. You get out and meet people, and you do things with people so you know the people you're trying to help.' I never realized how well he did that."

"He would say, 'Yeah, I'll do that, Dad,' and then he would pass it off, and we'd forget about it," Lois Klinefelter, Dave's wife, said.

After Brian Klinefelter was shot, the stories came pouring in. Stories like Czech's. Stories about people Brian had helped with his friendly manner and quick smile.

"I told Lois, I said, 'God, why didn't I know that ahead of time and praise him rather than chew on him?'" Dave said.

Dave Klinefelter eventually learned what kind of a man his son was. The questions that dogged him after that were about what made the three people in that white pickup different kinds of men.

Chapter Five

Doug Thomsen and His Family, 1996

BRIAN EDERHOFF and Kenneth Roering tried to process what they'd just seen as Thomas Kantor drove the pickup truck away from where the police officer stopped them.

"What the hell are you doing?" Ederhoff yelled. "You just shot a cop."

Kantor was frantic, wild-eyed. "I didn't wanna shoot nobody tonight," he said, waving the gun around.

He shoved the weapon back in his jacket pocket and gripped the wheel, blinking repeatedly. "I can hardly see 'cause of the gun flashes," he shouted.

Roering leaned away from Kantor and into Ederhoff. Ederhoff was holding onto the door of the truck to steady himself as Kantor floored it. Roering gripped the dashboard in front of him in shocked silence.

Ederhoff and Roering had watched Kantor pull the truck to the side of the road, wondering what he was going to do. They'd watched as the officer approached the window, told them they had snow covering their license plate and asked Kantor for his license and registration. They'd watched as Kantor said, "Sure," then reached into his pocket as if he was getting his wallet. They'd watched as Kantor whipped out the gun and fired several shots through the open window into the cop, then popped the clutch and peeled off before he was even done shooting.

The night had begun with a robbery. Now Ederhoff and Roering were accessories to the shooting of a police officer. Every police force in central Minnesota would be crashing down upon them. If caught, they were destined for long stays in prison—or worse, if Kantor tried to shoot his way out.

Earlier in the night, Kantor had seemed calm and self-assured. Now he seemed desperate and dangerous as he pulled the truck past a large retail distribution center and into the neighborhoods of northwest St. Cloud.

Kantor took a left onto a side street lined with two-story houses, but quickly found that it was a cul-de-sac and there was nowhere to go. He tried to make a U-turn, but the truck's turning radius was too wide. So he flung it into reverse and backed straight into a giant pile of snow a city plow had compressed in the middle of the cul-de-sac.

The rear wheels spun but would not grip.

"Get out and push," he ordered.

Roering and Ederhoff jumped to comply.

The two of them moved behind the truck, climbing on top of the snow pile. They placed their hands on the tailgate and dug their feet into the packed snow as much as they could and started to push without speaking.

Roering briefly thought about running. But Kantor still had the gun. He had given him and Ederhoff guns before the robbery, but they had left them in a brown paper bag on the floor of the truck.

The truck rocked but did not pull forward. The wheels, still spinning on the snow and ice, began to smoke and give off an acrid odor. Then the driver's side door swung open and Kantor got out and ordered Ederhoff to take the wheel.

Kantor and Roering, the strongest of the three, managed to push the truck out of the snow.

They clambered back into the truck, Roering on the passenger side and Ederhoff sliding over to let Kantor get back behind the wheel.

Kantor maneuvered them onto County Road 134 and farther into St. Cloud. He took another left, cutting through the parking lot of a convenience store. The trio watched as two cars went by. Then the truck pulled out onto Eighth Street.

Kantor glanced up at the rearview mirror.

"I think there's a cop following us," he said.

He sped up, then suddenly turned left onto another small side street, this one lined with one-story ranch houses.

"We're gonna have to ditch the truck," he said.

Kantor yanked the vehicle into the driveway of one of the houses and put it in park. The three of them clambered out, Roering grabbing the paper bag with the guns as he did so.

Roering spotted a police car down the road with its lights flashing.

"Cops," he hissed.

The three ran around to the opposite side of the house, shielding themselves from view.

Kantor was about fifteen feet in front of the other two. He turned and looked at them while still running. "Follow me," he said, gesturing with his arm.

Roering nodded, but as Kantor turned right and headed toward the backyard of one of the other houses, Roering kept going forward, making for a grove of trees. Ederhoff followed him. Whatever was going to happen to Kantor, he'd be alone.

* * *

AT HIS RANCH HOUSE on Bromo Avenue, Doug Thomsen was unwinding after a long day on his feet. After his usual eight-to-five shift at the barbershop he'd come home and cleared snow from his driveway. Then he cleared the driveways of an elderly neighbor and the couple across the street who were on vacation in Hawaii.

Thomsen sat on his bed with his shoes off, in a sweatshirt and jeans, watching a basketball game on television. Thomsen's love of basketball started early in life, and he'd passed it down to both of his kids, along with genes that gave them a natural aptitude for it.

His daughter, Leah, was seventeen and six-foot-three, a gifted player at Apollo High School and already committed to St. Cloud State University.

His son, Dan, at fourteen, was almost as tall.

Doug heard the front door open.

He could hear Leah, who had been at an Apollo hockey game, greet his wife, Connie, who was at the dining room table working on her nails.

Then Leah appeared in his bedroom door. "Hi, Dad, " she said. "Just wanted to let you know I'm home."

"How was the game?" Doug asked.

"Good," she said.

Leah grabbed the cordless phone and headed down to her room in the basement.

The front door remained unlocked. They were expecting Dan home from basketball practice any minute.

* * *

NEXT DOOR to the Thomsens, eighty-six-year-old Lillian Klawitter thought she heard a noise at her patio door. She rose slowly from her chair and went to check, flipping on an exterior light. No one was there.

Then she heard noises coming from the garage attached to her house. She walked through her kitchen to the door that led out there and flipped on the garage light.

As she started to open the door, it swung back violently into her, knocking her off her feet and onto the kitchen floor.

A wild-eyed young man with brown hair and a long flannel jacket burst in. "Where's your keys?" he shouted.

Klawitter lay on the floor, shaking. As she struggled to rise, the man started ransacking her kitchen, pulling out drawers and rummaging through them.

"Where's your keys?" he demanded. "I want your car."

He went into her living room, and Klawitter could hear the crinkle of newspapers and magazines as he searched her coffee table.

"I want your car keys," he screamed again.

Klawitter grabbed a chair and tried to use it to pull herself upright. Pain shot through her hip, which had slammed into the floor when she went down.

The man stomped back into the kitchen. Now he had a gun in his hand.

"Give me those goddamn keys or else, bitch," he yelled at her.

The look in the man's eyes shook Klawitter to her core. It was primal desperation, unlike anything she had ever seen. He was running from something—probably the police.

Still, something inside Klawitter recoiled at the idea of giving in to this person who had invaded her home. "It's not my car," she lied, crying. "I don't have the keys."

The man tensed; she could see his jaw clench. She put her arms over her head to shield herself.

Then she heard the man give out a yell of frustration. She peeked out to see him running out of the kitchen and into the garage. She could hear her garage door open and then shoes clomping through deep snow outside.

Grabbing the chair again, she pushed through the pain and dragged herself into a seated position. Then she grabbed the phone off the wall and, shaking and whimpering, dialed the first number that came to her head.

* * *

CONNIE THOMSEN was still sitting at the kitchen table when she heard a rapid, urgent pounding on her front door. She frowned. They were expecting Dan, but he wouldn't knock. Especially not like that.

She rose from her chair, but before she could walk to the door, it burst open and in stepped someone she had never seen before, a young man with unkempt hair and a scraggly beard, wearing a long flannel jacket. Snow covered his boots and the bottom of his black jeans.

"I need your car keys," he growled, taking a step toward Connie.

He was breathing heavily, and his hands were concealed in his jacket pockets.

Connie's first thought was the man must have been in some sort of car accident and needed help. But there was a hunted look in his eyes that frightened her. She turned and hurried down the hall toward the bedroom, calling out to her husband as she went. "Doug," she said. "Doug, there's a man here who needs you."

Inside the bedroom, Doug hit the mute button on the TV remote control. His brow furrowed, and he looked toward the open bedroom door. His wife's words were odd, but it was the way she said them that really caused his heart to pump faster and adrenaline to begin coursing through him. She sounded scared.

He swung his legs off the bed. Before he could stand up Connie came through the door, her eyes wide. Right behind her was a strange man with a small, black gun in his hand.

"I need your car," he said.

Connie turned around, and the gun was pointed right at her. She gasped.

Doug tensed. He had a split-second to figure out what was going on and what he should do. A rush of heat coursed through him, but then he felt strangely calm. "Okay, I'll get you the keys. You can have the car," Doug said. "Any car you want that we have."

Doug slowly moved in front of his wife, his hands spread out in front of him so the man could see he had no weapon and was not a threat.

The man kept the gun trained on him, motioning for Doug to start walking out of the bedroom.

Doug did, moving toward the kitchen, hoping with all his might that Leah would not hear anything and stay downstairs.

I need to protect my family, he thought.

* * *

DOWN IN HER BASEMENT room, Leah was talking to a boy from school when she heard her phone beep. "Hold on, Chris," she said. "I've got another call."

Leah pressed the call waiting button and immediately heard a person on the other end of the line crying.

"Hello?" she said.

"Come quick. Somebody has to come over now," the person said.

Leah recognized the voice through the tears. It was Lillian from next door. Her family had been helping the older woman with her groceries and her yard work since her husband died two years earlier.

"Lil, what's wrong," Leah said. "What is it?"

"Please come quick," Lillian said.

She was whimpering, crying. Leah wondered if she had fallen and hurt herself. She started moving toward the bedroom door.

"Okay, Lil, hang in there," Leah said. "I'll get my dad."

"No, right now," Lillian wailed. "You need to send someone right now." She hung up.

Leah started running up the stairs, two at a time, calling for her father, the cordless phone still in her hand.

"Dad," she said. "Dad, Lil needs you."

When she came to the top of the stairs and into the kitchen, Leah saw that the front door was open. The night was dark and still and she felt the frigid outside air wafting across the room.

"Dad, Lil needs you," she said again, wondering why no one was responding. "Dad, you have to come now 'cause something's wrong."

Then her father came out of his bedroom, walking slowly, with a dazed, almost dumbfounded look on his face. A man Leah didn't recognize was right behind him.

Her mom trailed both of them, her face similarly frozen in shock.

Leah raised the phone to her ear.

"Chris, just wait," she said, then lowered it.

She stood at the top of the steps as the three passed her in the kitchen. The stranger reached out and snatched the phone from her, and her nose caught a scent of stale cigarettes and gasoline from his flannel jacket.

"I've got the keys right here," her father told the man as they walked toward the entrance to the garage. "It's got a full tank of gas."

"You're coming with me," the man said to him. "You've got ten seconds to put on your boots and grab the keys."

Leah watched in disbelief as her father leaned down to tug on his boots, and the man began counting. By the time he got to six, Doug had them on and laced.

"Can I grab a coat?" her father asked. "It's like negative twenty out there."

"No," the man said, and gestured for Doug to go out the door into the garage.

Leah saw her father glance back and take one last look at her and her mother. Then the man slammed the door shut.

The sound snapped her mom out of a state of shock, as if a spell had been broken.

"You have to go out there and see if they took the car with the car phone in it," she told Leah.

But as Leah reached for the door, Connie grabbed her arm and pulled her back. "No, wait until they leave," she said.

They heard the car start, and then Leah opened the door and went out into the garage. The large garage door was open and the freezing night air blasted her in the face. Her mother's Ford Thunderbird, with the mobile phone in it, was gone.

She went back in and told her mom.

"Oh, my God, he took him," Connie said, gripping her face in consternation. "He had a gun, and he took him and I don't even know where they went."

She grabbed both of Leah's arms and locked eyes with her.

"You have to go next door and call 911," she said. "You have to go to Lil's."

Leah could feel her mother's whole body shaking.

She broke free and ran out of the garage and down the driveway, ignoring the stinging cold.

Down the road she could see the family car slowly skidding back and forth. It was terrible on ice and snow.

Lillian's garage door was also open. The lights were on and Leah could see that both of the doors to Lillian's car were ajar. That was unusual.

Leah went to the front door and pounded on it.

"Lil, it's Leah," she screamed. "It's Leah. Let me in."

The cold air burned Leah's throat. Her breath was coming in short, quick, bursts and she could hear her heart pounding in her ears.

Lillian came to the door, opened it, then screamed and slammed it shut again.

"Lil, it's *me*," Leah yelled. "It's Leah. I need to use your phone."

They were both hysterical.

Lillian opened the door again and this time let Leah in. Leah ran by her and went to the living room to get the phone.

"He threw me down," Lillian kept saying, tears in her eyes. "He threw me down. I think I broke my hip."

"Are you okay?" Leah said, as she started dialing 911.

"I don't know," Lillian said, sitting down on the edge of an armchair next to Leah.

She was shaking.

"Lil," Leah said, "he took my dad."

Then a 911 dispatcher was on the line, and Leah was relaying what happened.

Lillian slumped back into the chair, her head in her hands. "Oh, my God," she said. "Oh, my God."

* * *

IN THE THUNDERBIRD, Doug was driving. His kidnapper was in the backseat, with the gun trained on him.

The Thomsen house was at the end of a T-intersection in a usually quiet neighborhood that was crawling with cops. As the Thunderbird rolled out of the driveway, squad cars were visible down the road to the right and left.

"Go straight," the man ordered, and Doug tried to comply. He hit the gas, but the wheels spun on the ice, and the back end began to fishtail. Doug let off the gas, pumping it and hoping the wheels would catch.

"Don't mess with me, man," the kidnapper said. "Get this thing going. If I get shot, you get shot."

He sounded panicky. Doug glanced in the rearview mirror and saw the man's eyes wide and nostrils flaring.

Calm him down.

Doug took a deep breath and spoke slowly and clearly. "I'm not messing with you. This car's just bad on ice," he said. "It's rear-wheel drive. I'm revving it, it's just not going anywhere. Look at the RPMs."

Doug pointed one finger at the dashboard, doing it slowly and not moving the rest of his hand from the wheel so the man wouldn't misinterpret his actions. As long as the guy's adrenaline level was pumping, who knew what he would do.

The car finally crept out of the neighborhood and onto County Road 4, which was better plowed. The speedometer started creeping past thirty and forty miles per hour.

They moved northwest and spotted a couple more police cars on side streets.

Doug briefly considered flashing the hi-beams to signal them, or even driving toward them.

"Don't do anything stupid," the kidnapper said, as if reading his thoughts. "I mean it. I'll shoot you."

"Okay," Doug said. "You just tell me where to go."

"Turn right here," the man said.

Doug complied, maneuvering the Thunderbird onto a thin, straight country road. The road was lined with snow-filled ditches. Beyond those was nothing but white fields and scattered stands of trees. There were no street lights and no other car headlights in sight. Only porch lights from the occasional country house broke up the darkness.

Doug knew they were headed toward an intersection called "Five Points," in the direction of the tiny town of St. Stephen.

Out in the country, with no cops in sight, the man in the backseat seemed to relax.

"You got any money?" he asked Doug.

"No, I don't have any with me," Doug said, keeping his eyes forward. "We left in a hurry, remember?"

"Yeah, I guess we did," the man said.

Doug stole another glance in the rearview mirror and saw that the man had leaned back and was resting his head against the seat. The gun was still in his hand, but he looked relaxed, even tired.

"Boy, I guess it's been one hell of a Monday night, hasn't it?" the man said.

"Yeah, I guess it probably has," Doug said.

Doug wondered if the man might fall asleep. The road was straight as far as he could see.

Where are we going?

"You know, I could just jump out here any time," Doug said.

"No, you're going with me for a while," the man said.

* * *

BACK IN WESTWOOD near Doug's house, Minnesota Highway Patrol officer Roger Anhorn was on call when a dispatcher informed him that a St. Joseph police officer had been shot.

Anhorn immediately felt a sense of dread.

God, I hope it's not Brian.

He tried to push those thoughts aside as he suited up and got ready to join the manhunt. But it wasn't easy.

Anhorn and his family went to Atonement Lutheran Church, where almost everyone knew the Klinefelters. And Anhorn was closer to Brian than most. He'd helped foster Brian's love of law enforcement, bringing him on ride-alongs and trying to shepherd him into a job with the state patrol. He thought of himself as Brian's mentor.

Anhorn took a few deep breaths as he slipped his bulletproof vest over his head and secured its Velcro straps. He did not know yet who the wounded officer was, and he did not know what the officer's condition was. Better to focus on what he did know: Three guys in a white pickup were on the loose, one of them had shot a cop and the dispatcher said they were last seen heading toward his area of St. Cloud.

Then the phone rang again.

It was Connie Thomsen, and she was frantic.

"He took Doug! He took Doug!" she was screaming.

Immediately Anhorn knew the two events were connected. These guys were desperate, were on the run, and they had now kidnapped his good friend. In an instant, his priorities changed.

Anhorn handed off the phone to his wife, Linda. "Talk to Connie," he said. "I'm going to go get her and the kids and bring them over here."

As quickly as he could, he strapped his sidearm to his hip and pulled on his maroon Highway Patrol parka. Then he headed over to the Thomsens' house.

Roger and Linda had been close to the Thomsens for years. They had joined Atonement on the same day decades earlier and had gone to Bible studies together almost every week since.

They had all been on a weekend getaway to a bed and breakfast in Alexandria recently, and then the Thomsens had been over to the Anhorns' house just the day before for a Super Bowl party.

Anhorn shook his head at the unbelievable turn the night had taken. In the back of his mind a gnawing fear still remained that the officer who was shot was his friend Brian Klinefelter. But now he had to focus on the reality that his friend Doug Thomsen was being held hostage by the shooter.

Anhorn saw Connie Thomsen in his headlights before he even arrived at her house. She was in the middle of the street, frantically flagging him down. He slammed on the brakes and when he got out of the car, she ran to him.

"He took Doug," she said again, her eyes wide and teary.

Anhorn gripped her shoulders and looked straight into her eyes. "I know," he said. "You go get the kids, and I'll take you all back to my place. You stay with Linda, and I'll go find Doug. I'll bring him home."

Anhorn knew he was making a promise he might not be able to keep. At that moment he had no idea where Doug had been taken or what his captors planned to do with him. But he said what he thought Connie needed to hear.

Anhorn took Connie and the kids back to his house, where Linda was waiting. He shepherded them all into an upstairs bedroom.

"Just stay here. Lock all the doors," he said. "I'm gonna go out and find Doug."

As he turned to leave again, Connie grabbed his arm.

"Please bring Doug back home," she pleaded. "I can't go on without him."

"I will, Connie," Anhorn said. "I promise."

* * *

THE COUNTRYSIDE slipped by as Doug Thomsen kept driving north. He stole brief glances in the rearview mirror. His kidnapper wasn't breathing down his neck anymore, but he still thought it best not to look at him too long.

After Doug had driven north for about ten minutes with no cars in sight, the man leaned forward.

"Stop the car right here," he said. "You're going in the trunk."

"Okay," Doug said, his mind racing.

Getting in the trunk sounded like a very bad idea, but arguing with a desperate, armed man seemed worse.

Doug pulled off as far as he could on the right shoulder, which still left about half the car in the road. As he got out the front door with the gun trained on him, he could see it didn't much matter.

The area was deserted. No headlights in either direction. He could see a couple houses off in the distance, but no one was going to see what was happening to him from there.

The night was frigid and clear. Starlight illuminated the plumes of breath coming from both men's mouths.

"Open the trunk," the kidnapper ordered.

Doug complied, twisting the key in the lock and lifting the lid.

Inside were three giant bags of salt, 100 pounds each. They were Doug's attempt to keep a little more weight above the rear wheels so the car would grip better on snow and ice.

He stuck one leg in the trunk, but it was obvious he wouldn't be able to fold his entire tall frame inside next to the bags.

"Take those out," the man said, gesturing with the gun a bit impatiently.

Again Doug did as he was told, hoisting the bags out one by one and setting them on the side of the road. It gave him a little time to think, but no good options came to mind.

If he tried to run for one of those houses, there was no guarantee the man wouldn't shoot him. Plus, he was already shivering, and his fingers had gone numb. If no one was home he could die of hypothermia quite quickly out here.

"Do you have a coat?" the man asked.

"No," Doug said. "Remember, we left in a hurry. You didn't let me get a coat."

"Oh, yeah," the man said, nodding.

He had calmed down significantly.

Doug crawled into the trunk, his knees folded up against his chest. He shoved his hands under his arms for warmth.

The man stood there with one hand on the trunk lid and the other on his gun and looked down at him.

"You'll be okay," he said. Then he shut the trunk, and suddenly everything was pitch black.

Those last three words echoed in Doug's head.

You'll be okay.

You'll be okay.

You'll be okay.

What could he possibly mean?

The car started and lurched forward.

Doug could think of several scenarios in which the night ended with him not being okay. The car was hard to maneuver on ice even for someone who was accustomed to driving it. This man could easily wreck it and kill them both. Or he could ditch it somewhere and leave Doug in the trunk, where it was only slightly warmer than outside. In his sweatshirt and jeans, Doug knew he wouldn't last more than an hour or so.

What if the night ended with a car chase or a shootout with police? Doug wondered how thick the metal lining of the trunk was, and how much it would slow down a bullet.

He began to pray.

God of mercy, God of might, help me, get me through this night. God of mercy, God of might, help me, get me through this night. God of mercy, God of might, help me, get me through this night.

The chorus ran through his head over and over.

He tried to keep track of which direction they were headed, but after two or three turns, he was completely disoriented.

How am I going to get out of here if he ditches the car? What am I going to do?

There were large crossbeams across the backseat, so going back into the cabin of the car was not an option. He wondered about trying to kick the trunk latch and shifted his leg as much as he could, but the backs of the taillights protruded into his space and he couldn't get the leverage he would need.

Doug could feel the car slowing. He wondered if they were in a new town. It felt as if he had been in the trunk a long time, but he could not tell. Time and space had ceased to make sense in the dark confines of the freezing trunk.

He could feel the car suddenly slow even more and make a very sharp right turn. Oddly, it kept turning. Turning, turning, turning slowly, like they were on a freeway on-ramp. Then the car finally straightened out and sped up a little. Doug heard a hollow sound underneath the spinning wheels. He recognized it. *We just went over a bridge. Where are we?*

* * *

NANCY WIGGIN was working the night shift for the Benton County Sheriff's Department on January 29, 1996.

She heard about the liquor store robbery in Albany over the radio. But that was twenty miles away, outside her jurisdiction, and the situation seemed to have little bearing on her. She did not know the night's violence was creeping closer and closer to her as the minutes ticked by.

Wiggin was thirty-four and had joined the Benton County force two years earlier. She grew up in the southern suburbs of the Twin Cities and had always gravitated to male-dominated jobs: ambulance EMT, warehouse driver, security, and traffic control at Minneapolis' large international airport. Now cop.

She was at a tow yard that night, talking to some truck drivers who had been relatively busy. A lot of car engines were not built for that night's weather. Neither were humans. She was wearing her police-issued parka—one of the few times she could remember keeping it on for a full shift.

Another deputy trotted over to where she was chatting with the drivers, his breath making small clouds in the air. He looked agitated.

"Nancy, there's something going on in Stearns County," he said. "A burglary or robbery or something. Possible officer down. You gotta get on your scanner."

Wiggin jogged back to her squad car and shut the door. She removed her leather gloves, turned up the volume on her dispatch radio and blew into her hands to warm them.

An officer had been shot. Three white males in a white pickup truck had fled the scene, heading east. If they stayed on that path and crossed the Mississippi River, they'd be in Benton County.

She pulled the gloves back on, jerked her patrol car into drive and headed for the bridge in Sauk Rapids.

All was quiet there.

Another officer arrived to watch that spot, so she headed north for Rice. There was another bridge there.

As she went through the city of Sartell she came to a four-way stop near the large paper mill, one of the town's main employers. The mill sat on the river so huge trees could be floated down to be turned into paper. There was a bridge there, also, and no police were watching it. Wiggin parked her squad car near the intersection.

The radio traffic was relentless.

The three men had ditched their truck and set off on foot. Two of them split off and were running through yards. K-9 units were being dispatched to sniff them out of hiding.

The other one had busted into a house. He had taken a car at gunpoint, a champagne-colored Thunderbird. There was a hostage.

Wiggin shook her head. The night had gone crazy. She reached over to the passenger side of her squad car, opened the glove compartment and pulled out a map of St. Cloud and the surrounding area.

She knew approximately where the carjacking had occurred. She wanted to know how far she was from it.

Not far.

She put the map away and tried to focus. What did she need to look for? It was a champagne-colored Thunderbird. What did "champagne" mean? Beige? Light pink? Too much detail, she decided. Just look for a light-colored, late model Thunderbird. She knew some people who drove the newer T-Birds, and she had an idea of what the taillights looked like at night. That's what she would keep an eye out for.

She sat at the side of the road, facing the bridge on the opposite side of the intersection, drumming her fingers on the steering wheel as cars went by. There was a steady stream of traffic. More than she would have expected.

A light-colored car came up over the bridge and started to turn right onto Benton Drive. It looked like a T-Bird, but Wiggin couldn't be sure.

She craned her neck, hoping for a look at the license plate, but just then a pickup truck pulled up alongside her squad car and blocked the view temporarily.

The light-colored car rolled through the intersection and Wiggin caught a glimpse of the taillight design. It looked like what she was waiting for. After the pickup cleared the intersection she pulled into the street and turned left onto Benton Drive.

By then the car was about half a mile ahead, disappearing occasionally around bends in the curvy section of road. She didn't turn her lights or siren on. She wanted to get closer, get a better look at the vehicle and the license plate, to be sure she really had something before she called it in. She didn't want to needlessly add to the radio traffic, but if it was the right car, and there was an armed man with a hostage inside, she did not want to approach it by herself.

Wiggin pulled through a curve and into a straightaway and steadily depressed the accelerator. Her squad car pulled closer and closer to the vehicle ahead. The plate she was looking for was 187 KIP.

The car ahead passed under a bridge. When it emerged from the shadows on the other side, she was close enough to see the plate. She saw the letters first: KIP. The first number was obscured by snow, but the others looked like an eight and a seven. Wiggin felt a warm rush of adrenaline course through her neck. Five out of six was more than enough. She reached for her radio to call it in. "I'm in pursuit of hijacked vehicle," Wiggin said after identifying herself. "Heading south on Benton Drive between Sauk Rapids and Sartell."

* * *

ROGER ANHORN was driving around somewhat aimlessly. He was looking for Doug, but he didn't know where to look. Last he heard, Doug's car was heading north, so Anhorn started off toward Sartell.

He was praying the whole way.

God, lead me to where Doug is. Let me find him, let him be okay.

By then the kidnapper had been identified as a twenty-six-year-old named Thomas Kantor. Anhorn knew little about Kantor or his motives. He knew he was alone—the K-9 unit had cornered his two accomplices hiding under a deck. He knew Kantor had shot a police officer and was probably desperate.

Scenarios of what could happen to Doug began to play out in Anhorn's head, though he tried to push them away.

It was so dreadfully cold. What did this Kantor guy have in mind? Would he put Doug out of the car on some deserted road to freeze to death? Would he shoot him and then leave him buried in a snow-covered ditch?

How is this going to end? Am I going to find Doug? What kind of condition is he going to be in?

Anhorn's heart was racing, but there was nothing else he could do. He felt helpless. So he kept praying.

And then the call he was waiting for came over the radio. A Benton County deputy had spotted Doug's car and was in pursuit on Benton Drive in Sauk Rapids.

Anhorn was about five miles away. He flipped on his siren and punched the accelerator to the floor.

* * *

WIGGIN WATCHED as the car ahead began to slow. It swerved over to the shoulder, slowly, gradually, like someone just deciding to take a break from driving.

"He's pulling over," she told the dispatcher.

Wiggin dropped the radio and put both hands on the steering wheel, pulling her own car behind the parked Thunderbird. She was about three car-lengths away, and slightly staggered toward the road. She turned on the light bar above the car to warn passing motorists.

It was a fairly deserted area. To the west were train tracks and a park that ran along the river. Houses stood on the other side of the road, but they were up a snow-covered hill. The homes and businesses of downtown Sauk Rapids were still a few hundred yards up the road to the south.

What is he doing? Wiggin thought as she put her squad car in park and wriggled free of her seatbelt.

* * *

IN THE TRUNK Doug was still praying—and trying to figure out where he was.

After the bridge noise, there had been another right turn. The car continued at a steady but not particularly fast pace.

Doug could feel the tip of his nose and his earlobes going numb, but there was nothing he could do to warm them. Just when he was beginning to wonder if he would freeze in the trunk, the car pulled slightly to the right and slowed to a stop.

What's happening?

* * *

WIGGIN OPENED the driver's-side door and pulled her gun from its holster as she got out. The .45-caliber Smith and Wesson felt heavy in her hand.

The driver's-side door of the car ahead of her also opened, and someone clad in jeans and a flannel jacket clambered out. She glanced into the car, but her radio was now out of reach. She fumbled with her lapel radio, but couldn't get a signal.

In training Wiggin had been taught to use her car door as protective cover if she was threatened during a traffic stop. So she crouched behind the open door and watched through the window, pointing her gun through the V-shaped space the door made.

The man in flannel was average height and weight, with brown hair. He was unremarkable except for the small black object in his hand that glinted in the light of the streetlamps.

It looked like a pistol, a semi-automatic. He was holding it down by his side, almost casually.

"Drop the gun," Wiggin yelled.

She could feel her heart pounding. Her hand clenched around the handle of the Smith and Wesson, her finger poised over the trigger.

The man started walking alongside the Thunderbird toward her, stone-faced. The gun stayed in his hand.

* * *

IN THE DARKNESS of the trunk, Doug strained to hear what was going on. He had heard a female voice yell for someone—he supposed it was his kidnapper—to drop his gun. There was a firmness, an authority to the voice that instantly told him it had to be a police officer. His heart pounded as he waited to hear the response.

Footsteps crunched in the snow, one after another, all of them now seeming to come from behind the car.

Thirty seconds that felt like an eternity passed. Then the female voice rang out again. "Drop the gun," the speaker said again, this time with more of an edge to it.

All was quiet for a second, and then Doug heard a loud, unmistakable pop.

Someone had fired a shot. But who?

Doug lay as still as possible, breathing quickly and shallowly. Outside, there was no sound.

Then the stillness was rent by sirens and the sounds of tires grinding to a halt against the snow and more radios squawking and people talking hurriedly.

Friendly voices, Doug thought.

He started pounding on the door of the trunk.

"Has anyone secured that vehicle?" a male voice yelled.

Several voices answered, "No."

Footsteps crunched toward Doug, getting louder.

"Just a moment, we'll get you out of there," a slightly less-muffled voice said from the other side of the trunk.

"I'm Doug Thomsen. I own this car," Doug yelled. "There's a silver button on the console you can push, and the trunk will pop, or take the key out of the ignition and open it that way."

He heard the engine stop, then heard the key in the trunk lock.

"Make sure your hands are visible," the voice said. "And do not, under any circumstances, make any sudden moves."

Doug had seen enough cop shows on TV to know what that meant. In the dark, he put his hands out in front of his chest and did his best to stop shivering.

Then the trunk swung open, and he was temporarily blinded by flashlights and the blinking red and blue of several squad cars. He squinted. As his eyes adjusted, he saw six guns of various types pointed at him, all them held by uniformed police officers.

"God, am I glad to see you," Doug said.

Gradually, the guns lowered.

Arms reached out to him and several of the officers helped him climb out of the trunk. He wobbled a bit as he tried to stand, a combination of leg cramps and ebbing adrenaline overtaking him.

"You all right, sir?" one of the officers said.

"Yeah, I think so," Doug answered, placing his hand on his car to steady himself.

Another car with flashing lights arrived on the scene, snow crunching under its tires as it came to an abrupt stop.

Roger Anhorn jumped out of the driver's-side door and jogged toward Doug, who had never been happier to see his friend. A newspaper photographer who had also just arrived snapped pictures as the two hugged on the side of the road in the glare of a dozen headlights.

Minutes later, Roger made the joyous call to his house to let Connie know he'd kept his promise. He'd found Doug, he was okay and he would be coming home.

Neither man noticed Nancy Wiggin crouched nearby over the body of a young man in a flannel shirt.

The man would not drop the gun. He and Wiggin had circled around her squad car, him approaching and her backpedaling, trying to keep some metal between them. At one point he had raised the gun to his own temple. Then he started to lower it in her direction and she fired, center mass, like she'd been taught.

The single shot felled him.

Blood was coming from a hole in his chest, running down his jacket and pooling in the snow around him.

She reached down to touch his neck. She couldn't feel a pulse. She removed the glove from her right hand and reached down to try again, but another officer put his hand on her shoulder and led her away so others could begin to render aid.

Wiggin suddenly felt light-headed and very tired. Her shoulders slumped as she let the other deputy lead her back toward her car.

"I didn't want to shoot him," she said. "But I had to."

Chapter Six

Doug Thomsen,
Nineteen Years Later

ALMOST TWENTY YEARS after he was rescued, Doug Thomsen stood in front of a class of criminal justice students at St. Cloud State University and told them his story.

The students sat in silence in the nondescript classroom, listening as Doug told them about the fear in his wife's voice, the odd calm that helped him guide the car as Thomas Kantor held a gun on him, and the surreal scene of a half-dozen guns pointed at him through the haze of exhaust billowing from the squad cars' tailpipes into the frost-tinged night.

Doug liked helping the next generation of police, but he'd found that talking about his abduction helped him, too.

"This is good therapy for me," he told the students.

Stewart Wirth, a criminal justice professor at SCSU, sat at his desk and observed while Doug held the students' attention at the front of the room.

This was not Doug's first time talking to Wirth's class. But this time he'd brought Connie, who teamed with Doug to field questions about the experience after he was done.

One of the students, a young woman, had a comment rather than a question. "I have goosebumps on my arms thinking about what your family went through that night," the student said, her eyes wide. "I've known for some time that this is the line of work I want to do, but you just confirmed why I really want to do this. I really hope I have the opportunity to make a difference in someone's life."

* * *

PROFESSOR WIRTH is a former lieutenant in the Wright County Sheriff's Department and a friend of Roger Anhorn. The two of them teamed up to do critical incident stress debriefings in fourteen counties during their law enforcement days. For over ten years they talked to people who had been through all manner of trauma, trying to get them to process and explain what happened both for the official record and for the interview subject's emotional well-being.

"We've done everything up to and including officers killed in the line of duty and officers involved in shootings as well," Wirth said.

When Wirth first started teaching his class at St. Cloud State University in 2004, it was called "Interview and Interrogations." He immediately separated the two topics because he didn't want his students to meld the two ideas in their minds. The techniques they use to interview the victims of crime should be vastly different from those they employ when interrogating suspects, Wirth explained.

In his first decade of teaching, Wirth saw a troubling trend in his students. As they became more adept at communicating through technology like texting and emailing, they became less experienced at carrying on face-to-face conversations. They were less able to pick up on changes in facial expressions and tones of voice that could clue them in to how their questions were being received—an invaluable skill when interviewing a victim of violent crime.

That's where Doug Thomsen came in.

Wirth had spent many hours getting his hair cut in Doug's chair over the years, and the two talked as people often do in the barbershop. Every January the talk turned to that bitterly cold night when Doug's quiet life had been briefly shattered.

Eventually Wirth asked Doug if he would come to his class and tell his students the story. Doug agreed to do it.

"The conversation in the barber's chair was more one-on-one, but when he made the decision to come into my classroom and share, that's a whole different thing," Wirth said. "I saw that part of the journey being positive for him, and he's told me that."

Talking about that night helped Doug continue to purge himself of the fear and trauma of being held at gunpoint and not knowing what would happen.

At the same time, it helped Wirth's students understand what it was like to be victimized in that way and helped them interact with other victims in the future.

Wirth called it "preparing the next watch." Doug has talked to more than 100 students, most of whom would go on to be police officers, probation officers, corrections officers, or other law enforcement professionals.

"The first time they have a conversation with someone who has been through something like that should not be for real in the street," Wirth said. "They should have an opportunity to listen to that kind of a story from someone in a classroom setting."

And so they did. They listened attentively and then dug into the story and asked questions. They watched how Doug reacted and got a feel for which parts of the story were most difficult for him to recount.

Doug Thomsen and Stewart Wirth are on the cutting edge of what Wirth calls a "sea change" in Minnesota law enforcement.

Wirth said the licensing manual for the Minnesota Peace Officers Standards and Training Board, which certifies officers throughout the state, was changed for 2015. For the first time it emphasized, at the very top of its list of "core competencies," human communication.

Wirth said he'd been emphasizing that side of law enforcement for years, passing along the lesson of a former patrol sergeant who sat him down when he was a rookie and told him, "The muscle that you're going to use the most is the one in your jaw."

But talking about interviewing victims of crime and actually talking to a victim of crime are different experiences. So Wirth keeps inviting Doug Thomsen to speak to his classes.

"Doug will do this for me as long as he's comfortable doing it," Wirth said.

Every year Doug Thomsen helps train the next generation of police officers to be more like Brian Klinefelter—to have his people skills and "gift of gab."

* * *

DOUG'S TALKS also have been a tribute to his friends in law enforcement, some he knew before that night in 1996 and some he met because of it.

Bob Bushman was a young, square-jawed officer with the Minnesota Bureau of Criminal Apprehension when he took Doug under his wing after he was rescued that night.

Doug went from the trunk of his car to the backseat of a squad car and then to a local police station bustling with agitated cops. He was able to call his family and tell them he was okay, but was instructed not to talk about what had happened until after he was questioned.

Bushman was the one who took him into a side room for questioning and told him what else happened that night: that the man who abducted him was Thomas Kantor, that before coming to his house Kantor had shot a police officer and that two men who had been with Kantor at the time had been captured in his neighborhood.

Decades later, Doug still remembers how stunned he was. He thought Kantor was nothing more than a car thief.

Doug said that the following twenty-four hours were the most difficult for him, as the adrenaline subsided and he realized just how much danger he had been in. Those hours would have been even harder if not for Bushman.

Doug remembered running through the events of that night in the interview room and second-guessing himself. What if he had plowed the car into a snowbank, or tried to run when Kantor made him get out and get in the trunk?

"Did I do the right thing?" Doug asked Bushman.

"You did everything perfectly," Bushman reassured him. "You know how I know? You're sitting here right now."

Bushman then gently briefed him on what to expect next: he would be questioned, he would have to give statements and relive his kidnapping many times over. There would be legal proceedings for Kantor's accomplices that could drag on for years. And for the next few days the media would be hounding Doug and his family.

"By talking to the press yourself, when you're ready," Bushman told him, "you can shield your wife and kids."

When Bushman drove Doug home late that night, sure enough, a television van was parked on the street outside. Bushman offered to shoo the reporter away, but Doug remembered approaching the reporter and kindly but firmly telling him he just wanted to spend the night with his family.

The next day Doug got a call from Al Catello, an FBI agent who was also one of his barbershop customers.

"Hey, cowboy, what the hell are you trying to do, round up the bad guys?" Catello said. "That's my job."

Doug laughed. "Al, you can have your job," Doug said. "I'm not interested in it."

Doug then remembered Catello immediately getting serious. He asked about Doug's state of mind and asked how Connie and the kids were doing.

"Listen to me," Catello said. "I don't know if anybody has told you this yet, but you're going to need some counseling. You're going to have to get debriefed on this thing. We all do."

Doug and the whole family went to counseling with a therapist who served law enforcement agencies. It helped.

One of the things the therapist told them, Doug said, is that anger over what happened that night would only hurt them. It would keep them from moving on.

So Doug did his best to let go of any anger.

He did not avoid thinking or talking about that night. He did not change the way he viewed the world. Doug Thomsen locks his doors at night, but still leaves them unlocked when he's home during the day.

"I don't live in fear," Doug said.

Friends asked if he would've shot Thomas Kantor that night if he had a gun in his bedroom. Doug considered it in a clinical, non-emotional way. He might have, to protect his family, but the weapon would have had to be cocked and loaded in his hand.

"It happened that fast," Doug said.

Doug said he later talked to Thomas Kantor's middle school principal, who described Kantor as one of the few students he ever feared. Kantor, the principal said, showed no remorse when caught breaking rules.

But when Doug talks about Thomas Kantor now, he does so with no malice. He wonders why Kantor asked him if he had any warm clothes before he ordered him into the trunk, and why he told him, "You'll be okay."

He thinks Kantor had made up his mind that he would die that night, but perhaps had enough compassion not to force Doug to die with him.

For the other two, Doug also has no anger. They didn't come to his door that night, and Doug doesn't seem to hold it against them that that didn't stop Kantor from doing so.

"Those two guys were probably real followers," Doug says. "Tom Kantor was the leader of the whole thing."

Doug still has deep emotions about that night, but they are related to what others went through.

He says the hardest thing now is thinking about his family, and the hell Connie and the kids were in for that hour while he and Kantor were driving around.

The trauma hit Leah hard.

After Connie sent Leah next door to use Lillian Klawitter's phone, Connie ran outside to try to flag down a police car. When Leah returned from Lillian's, the house was empty. She did not know where her mother was. By then police were up and down the block and the neighborhood was alive with activity. A neighbor found Leah on her knees in the garage, crying and screaming for her mom and dad.

It was harder to tell how the experience had affected Dan. Like most fourteen-year-old boys, he was still developing a vocabulary for sharing his feelings, and he was reticent by nature anyway.

But as he and Doug sat in a car together a week later, Dan placed his hand on Doug's knee and said, "Dad, were you scared?"

Doug looked at his son and saw lurking in that short question all sorts of other questions about how Dan felt when he came home that night and his father was missing, and about what it meant to be a man.

"You're darn right I was scared," Doug said, and squeezed his son's arm.

In his fear, Doug turned to prayer.

Doug was a regular churchgoer, but he was not a man who wore his faith on his sleeve. There was no fish symbol outside his barbershop and he didn't try to evangelize to his customers.

But he was public about turning to God while he was trapped in that trunk. "I prayed real hard," he told a *St. Cloud Times* reporter. "I prayed to God to deliver me from that night and protect my family. He answered my prayers. I believe that's what saved me that night."

As he addresses the students at St. Cloud State he tells them that, at the time he was kidnapped, Connie was being treated for lymphoma, going through rounds of chemotherapy.

Doug tells them he was praying regularly that he would have at least five more years with his wife. Now nineteen years later, Connie is still with him, cancer-free.

"I don't know what I'm going to do for God now," Doug says, grinning.

That night in the trunk made Doug appreciate every day with Connie even more. It made him appreciate seeing his children grow into adults. Watching Dan help Lillian—who lived several more years after that night—get her groceries and drive her to appointments. Watching Dan become a father and name one of his children Lillian after his feisty former neighbor.

Leah is married with children now, too, and she has a master's degree in English education. As part of her coursework, she wrote a paper about that night and what she felt.

Leah was a classmate of Jacob Wetterling, an eleven-year-old boy who was riding his bicycle in St. Joseph with his brother and a friend in 1989 when a stranger stopped the three boys and took Jacob.

Jacob has not been found.

That was Leah's concept of kidnapping when her father was taken seven years later. Someone storms into your life and takes you, and your family never sees you again. That was what she feared when her father was kidnapped.

But her essay about that night ended triumphantly, with her family hugging each other close in the early hours of the morning, and she and Dan pulling their blankets and pillows into their parents' room to sleep near the foot of the bed where Doug and Connie lay.

She wrote about how they prayed together as a family, and then she and Dan fell asleep to the reassuring sound of their parents whispering to each other.

"All I know is that this family is stronger tonight," Leah wrote. "We cannot be split apart."

Nineteen years later, Doug can remember the way his two children folded their unusually tall bodies onto the floor and how it felt to have all the Thomsens together again.

Doug's family was secure. The trauma of that night had not broken them, but brought them closer together. But years later he thought he had more to give, that the experience could bring about some good in the law enforcement community, as well.

He remembered something Bob Bushman told him as he drove him back to his house that night.

Bushman said he wished the night had never happened, but focusing on Doug getting home helped him get through that night, and inspired him to keep going through unceasing days of chasing drug dealers, rapists, and murderers through the dark corners of society that most people would rather not see.

"I don't often get an opportunity to deal directly with victims and somebody I can really help," Bushman told Doug. "It really makes me feel good I'm able to take someone like you and reunite you with your family tonight. That's kind of why I do this job."

So Doug goes to St. Cloud State and tells the criminal justice students about how a police officer could find something rewarding about the job even on one of its darkest, coldest nights.

He also tells his story to future law enforcement officers in part because of what he saw after he got out of that trunk.

He saw his kidnapper, laying facedown on the snow in a pool of blood and later, at the police station, he saw a young female officer with a distant look in her eyes and an empty gun holster at her side.

Doug knew immediately what that meant. That was the officer who had shot his kidnapper and possibly saved his life. When he tried to thank her, she just gave him a wan smile.

He could tell her mind was elsewhere.

At the time Doug could not have known how that night would affect Nancy Wiggin or his good friend Roger Anhorn. But now he knows and it's become one of the most difficult parts of the story for him—as difficult emotionally as his own family's trauma.

Nineteen years later, Doug retraced the route he took with Kantor. He parked his Buick near the spot where he heard the gunshots from inside the trunk.

He told the story easily, matter-of-factly, until he got to the part where he was talking to Anhorn later that night, after they learned it was Brian Klinefelter who was shot.

Doug said he asked Anhorn how Klinefelter was doing and Anhorn couldn't speak. He just stood, silently, with tears welling in his eyes, then shook his head.

Recounting his friend's sorrow, Doug's head bowed over the Buick's steering wheel, and he, too, began to weep.

Chapter Seven

Roger Anhorn,
Nineteen Years Later

NHORN LIVES in Alexandria now, so he sees Doug Thomsen less than he used to.

"But whenever we do get together, it's like we haven't been apart," Anhorn said. "Doug and I have both said that this incident will bond us for life. It's something we share."

Finding Doug alive and well was one of the most joyous moments of Anhorn's life. But it was quickly followed by one of the most awful moments, when he learned that the St. Joseph officer who was shot was indeed Brian Klinefelter.

He had helped start Brian's law enforcement career, after all, and Brian helped revive his.

Anhorn had started with the Minnesota State Patrol in 1971. For many years he worked the overnight shift, from 10:00 p.m. to 6:00 a.m., and by the 1980s the job was starting to warp his perception of the younger generation.

"I eventually got kind of a twisted view of what the youth were," Anhorn said, looking back, "because I ran into all the bad ones."

His wife suggested he get involved with Atonement Lutheran Church's youth group.

Anhorn bonded quickly with the Atonement kids, and his jaded feelings about young people slowly melted into something more nuanced, more individualized. In retrospect, he said, that helped him do his job better.

The youth group was also where he met Brian.

Brian was among a group of forty Atonement kids who went to a national Christian conference in Colorado one year. Anhorn was a chaperone, in charge of about ten of them.

The first few days went by without incident. But on Sunday, the day of the conference's main rally, the Denver Broncos happened to be playing a pre-season game at a stadium nearby.

Brian and about five other teenage boys skipped out on the rally to go to the football game instead. As punishment, they had to stay in their hotel room that night while the rest of the group went to the dance that wrapped up the conference.

Anhorn volunteered to stay behind and keep an eye on them.

The boys quickly turned their punishment into pleasure, getting Anhorn to tell them old war stories about being a state trooper. They weren't interested in hearing about the paperwork.

"They wanted all the gruesome, exciting parts," Anhorn said, chuckling at the memory.

Across the street from their high-rise hotel was a building that was being remodeled and appeared to be empty.

But in the middle of Anhorn's stories, one of the boys saw something and called everyone over to the window. There were flashlight beams moving in the dark of the building across the street, and silhouettes of what looked like people running.

Anhorn surmised that someone might be burglarizing or vandalizing the place, and they called the local cops.

"These kids were just all excited about being a part of reporting this possible crime," he remembered.

One of them was Brian Klinefelter, who already had an interest in law enforcement. Getting to know Anhorn only strengthened it.

Anhorn stayed close as Brian grew up and went to Alexandria Technical and Community College to study criminal justice. When Brian came back to St. Cloud on breaks, he would ask Anhorn if he could go on ride-alongs with him.

"I said, yeah, that's fine," Anhorn recalled. "I'll show you what we do. We just had a great rapport, and I was just more and more impressed with the quality of individual he was."

By the time Brian got done with school, Anhorn was convinced he would make a great state trooper, and Brian was interested in the job. But there was a hiring freeze at the state level at the time.

A couple years later the state was hiring, and Anhorn urged Brian to apply, saying he would write him the most glowing recommendation he possibly could. But by then Brian was already working for the St. Joseph Police Department. He hadn't been on the job very long, and he felt a responsibility to stay with the department that gave him his first shot and trained him for at least a little while.

Brian was dedicated to St. Joseph, which was how he ended up on that dark, cold road that night, pulling over Thomas Kantor, when he was supposed to be off the clock.

Anhorn said he still feels some burden of guilt over what happened that night, some sense of responsibility for fostering Brian's love of law enforcement.

But he said the sense of guilt would be much worse if not for Brian's parents and Wendy. He apologized to them, tearfully, after Brian was shot, but they would have none of it.

Instead they thanked him for helping him live his law enforcement dream.

Their quiet Christianity inspired him and others.

"The faith was alive and well and demonstrated over and over again by that whole family," Anhorn said. "It's just absolutely amazing and they're the same way today. It's what got us all through that difficult process."

He paused.

"I said an awful lot of prayers in that healing process myself," he added.

Anhorn also drew strength from joining other police officers in building a house for Brian's young family.

Huge numbers of law enforcement officers turned out for the build, as he recalled.

"We spent a lot of hours out there, building that home, but I tell you, what a healing process that was, being able to help Brian fulfill one of his dreams," Anhorn said. "I still kinda tear up when I think about it."

After Brian's shooting, Anhorn returned to his job with a refreshed sense of the risks he faced. He and his wife would acknowledge that every time he left for work it might be the last time they'd see each other.

He finished his career after thirty years with the state patrol—thirteen on the road and seventeen in administration.

Chapter Eight

Nancy Wiggin,
Nineteen Years Later

FOR OTHERS INVOLVED the night Brian Klinefelter was shot, it was the beginning of the end of their law enforcement journey.

Nancy Wiggin's shooting of Tom Kantor was deemed justified. Hardly anyone in the community at large questioned her actions that night. Many hailed her as a hero.

But she wanted no accolades, no attention. After that night, she didn't want to be a police officer anymore.

Anhorn and others are convinced that Tom Kantor forced her to pull the trigger—that his death was a classic "suicide by cop."

"If somebody wants to take their own life, as unfortunate as that is, that's bad enough," Anhorn said. "But when you affect somebody else's life for the rest of their life by forcing them to kill you because you wanna die, what a horrible thing to do. And Nancy's just a living example of that."

* * *

NINETEEN YEARS LATER, it's hard to piece together how Nancy Wiggin is doing.

She quit the force shortly after the shooting—that much was widely known.

The rest trickled out second– and third-hand: she works in a factory in St. Cloud. She lives above a grocery store in a small town in central Minnesota. She doesn't talk about the shooting.

A letter addressed to Wiggin sent to the grocery store went unanswered. An in-person visit was the last resort.

The drive up was pleasant, with little traffic on a four-lane highway lined by evergreen trees.

Off the highway, the exit turned into a long, local street lined by small houses with big yards adorned by old trees.

The grocery store was easy to miss—two stories, but not much wider than any of the other storefronts.

Inside were a few tightly packed aisles of dry goods and a wall of coolers along the side. The clerk on duty, a middle-aged woman, nodded when asked if Nancy Wiggin lived upstairs. She left the register untended briefly and headed through a door in the back, revealing a narrow staircase.

Moments later she returned.

"She's not answering the door," she said, smiling apologetically. "She might be asleep."

She promised to give Wiggin a letter next time she saw her.

Months passed and there was still no response from Wiggin.

Others who knew her said she was not going to respond. They said the law enforcement part of her life was behind her and that was where she wanted to leave it.

Stewart Wirth, who debriefed other officers who had to shoot someone, was not surprised.

"Some people do not recover," Wirth said. "That's just the bottom line. Some people just don't make it back. We do everything we can to try to support folks who have been involved in that, but it's a life-changing thing."

For the officers who worked most closely with Brian Kline-felter, the night he was shot was also life-changing, and the road to recovery long.

Chapter Nine

Brad Lindgren, 1996

B RAD LINDGREN, chief of the small St. Joseph police force, was getting to Brian Klinefelter as fast as he could. Since the call came through about the robbery in Albany, his officers had been looking for white pickups, creating a dragnet that would catch the robbers if they tried to venture through St. Joseph.

Lindgren was at home when Sergeant Jeff Young called.

"Get up here right away," Young said. "Brian's been shot."

Lindgren grabbed his keys and yanked on a coat. His wife handed him his gun belt and bulletproof vest as he headed out the door. He threw them on the passenger seat of his truck and peeled out of his driveway.

Within minutes, Lindgren was at the shooting scene. It was controlled chaos.

Several firefighters and a woman who said she was a nurse were crouched over Brian's prone figure, performing CPR.

A Gold Cross ambulance was parked on the shoulder, sirens blaring and lights flashing. EMTs had placed a backboard under Brian.

A deputy from Stearns County, who said he'd been coming to back up Klinefelter, was on the scene as well.

A gray Chevy Nova was parked off to the side.

Brian was pale, unresponsive. Blood had pooled around his neck, spilling over the backboard and onto the pavement below.

The group of first responders gathered around to try to help the EMTs lift Brian into the ambulance, but the board wouldn't budge. Brian's blood had frozen between the backboard and the ground.

Everyone gripped the board, then tried again on the count of three. As they strained, Lindgren could hear the ice blood cracking.

The board came loose, and the EMTs began lifting Brian into the ambulance.

"Stop CPR," one of them said.

"NO!" Lindgren bellowed. "Continue CPR."

Everyone turned and looked at him.

"Just until we get him in the rig," an EMT explained.

Lindgren took a deep breath, raised both of his hands in the air and took a step back. "Listen to Gold Cross," he said.

The EMTs slid Klinefelter into the back of the ambulance, then one of them clambered up beside him.

"We need help in here for the transport," he said, looking back at Lindgren.

The firefighters were standing around, watching.

Lindgren grabbed one and thrust him toward the ambulance. He grabbed a second and did the same, almost throwing him into the back of the emergency vehicle. "They need help in there," he said.

Lindgren had gripped a third firefighter's jacket when he felt a hand rest gently on his shoulder. He turned and was face-to-face with the fire captain.

"Brad," the captain said gently, holding his gaze.

"Yeah?" Lindgren said impatiently.

"Brad, if you throw another fireman into that rig they won't be able to move," the captain said.

Lindgren stepped back again.

"Okay," he said, nodding. "You guys gotta do your job."

The doors shut and the ambulance pulled away, sirens blaring. Lindgren was left standing with two officers near the pool of frozen blood on the side of the road, next to an abandoned oxygen tank and other medical supplies.

A bit farther down the road another officer had taken a young woman out of his squad car and was walking her toward the Chevy Nova.

Her cheeks were streaked with tears that had formed crystals in her eyelashes before they fell. She looked stunned.

"What are you doing here?" Lindgren asked her.

She stared at him for a moment. "I just didn't want him to get run over," she mumbled, gesturing toward the Nova.

Lindgren noticed then how the car was parked diagonally, shielding the spot where Brian's body had been.

He felt a quick welling of gratitude toward the girl, who did not look much younger than Brian's wife, Wendy.

Wendy.

One of the other St. Joseph Reserve officers, a good friend of Brian's, walked over to Chief Lindgren.

"Brad," he said. "We've got to get over to Wendy's house."

"I know," Lindgren said.

Lindgren arranged for one of the deputies to secure the scene, then got on his radio to call for help in gathering evidence and taking the girl in to give a statement.

He left his truck there, getting in one of the squad cars with the reserve officer to drive over to Brian and Wendy's apartment in Sartell. On the way there the radio crackled with news of home invasions, an assault on an elderly woman, and the kidnapping of her neighbor.

"What the hell is going on tonight?" Lindgren said. "It's twenty below zero. It's usually deathly quiet."

By the time they parked in front of the Klinefelters' apartment, it was becoming clear that all of the events were linked. Police were now setting up a dragnet around St. Cloud to try to hem in the kidnapper.

Lindgren had gotten out of the squad car and was trudging toward the apartment door, trying to think of what he was going to say to Wendy, when the reserve officer swung open his car door.

"Brad," he yelled. "Nancy's got a vehicle stopped with the suspect in it." He gave the location, near the Bridge of Hope in Sauk Rapids on the river road. Less than a mile from the apartment complex.

"Oh, my God," Lindgren said. "Everybody's in St. Cloud. She's alone."

He ran back to the car and jumped in. The reserve officer hit the lights and sirens, and they rushed to the scene.

Lindgren tried to prepare mentally for a high-stakes standoff with a dangerous criminal. He realized he was in plainclothes, without his badge, in another county where officers would not necessarily recognize him as an ally.

He punched the radio and warned the dispatcher that he was not in uniform, but responding.

They arrived at the same time as other squad cars. In a flurry of flashing lights and tires crunching on snow, they came to an abrupt halt behind a champagne-colored Ford Thunderbird.

Lindgren saw a female officer in a parka with a gun still trained on a prone figure lying next to her squad car.

For the second time in a half-hour, Lindgren found himself staring down at a man sprawled out in the snow, with a pool of red forming under him. The wound was so fresh steam rose from the spilled blood into the frigid air.

After Doug Thomsen emerged from the trunk of the Thunderbird, his eyes wide at the guns trained on him, a Gold Cross ambulance arrived to take away the man who had been shot.

By then the TV news crews had gathered and were recording. The Sauk Rapids police chief had yet to arrive, so Lindgren took charge.

"Set up a perimeter," he said, grabbing a deputy by the arm. "Run a mile down there and push them away. This is a crime scene."

By the time that was done, he had gotten word from another St. Joseph officer that Wendy had been notified Brian was shot and was on her way to the hospital.

There was little for Lindgren to do but head there, too.

There was more radio traffic on the drive over. The other two men from the white truck had been tracked down by dogs. They were hiding under a deck near where they ditched the truck and did not put up a fight when cornered by scores of police.

The night was starting to calm down, and Lindgren's mind was turning to what he would face when he got to the hospital.

The emergency room lobby was crowded with cops from several different agencies by the time he got there. They were stoic, somber. A doctor had already come out and said there was nothing more he could do.

Brian Klinefelter was dead.

Lindgren stood looking down at the floor and shaking his head. A mixture of rage and deep sadness roiled inside him.

"What about the suspect?" a sergeant from the Stearns County Sheriff's Office asked the doctor.

"I'm afraid he's also expired," the doctor said.

Lindgren looked up, seething.

"Fuckin' good," he said.

The doctor's eyes narrowed in disgust and he turned and stomped out.

Nurses behind the ER desk eyed Lindgren with more sympathy as he collapsed into a chair, wondering how the night had gone so horribly wrong.

Chapter Ten

Brad Lindgren,
Nineteen Years Later

To get to Brad Lindgren's house nineteen years later, one had to drive the country roads directly south of St. Cloud into Meeker County.

Lindgren's gravel driveway was long and lined with trees on both sides. A small pond glimmered on the right. It was quiet, idyllic, far removed from the mayhem and gunfire of the night that took Brian Klinefelter's life.

Inside, Lindgren had dug up all of his records of that day and its aftermath. He retrieved a large plastic tub full of newspaper clippings, police trade magazines, and other write-ups about Brian, including the day he was honored by President Bill Clinton.

The shooting still does not make sense to him, in a lot of ways. It was one of those frigid nights when nothing usually happens because everyone is holed up at home. And Brian was supposed to be going off duty early.

But within an hour there had been an armed robbery, a kidnapping, and two shooting deaths, and Lindgren had been at the scene right after both shootings.

"That was just really weird and the ironic part for me," he said, shaking his head at the improbability.

Lindgren was still solidly built and his light brown hair and mustache had only a few streaks of gray. He still looked like he could respond to a call for backup, but he was retired after finishing his law enforcement career as Meeker County's chief deputy.

People still called him out of the blue to ask for advice every now and then. Sometimes they didn't even give their name. Lindgren had given out his cell phone number to a lot of troubled kids when he was a cop. Part of the job.

Investigating and compiling detailed reports on homicides was also part of the job, but it was different when the victim was his friend.

He remembered being in the hospital, next to Brian's body, as a forensics expert went over Brian's wounds one by one, showing him where the bullets entered and which one was fatal.

"It was like, 'ugh, I really don't want to hear this right now,' but he was doing a good job," Lindgren said.

In the days that followed, Lindgren remembered an already close St. Joseph community made closer. People came by the police station bearing food or special pictures and flowers. Lots of flowers.

"There was a lot of visiting," Lindgren said. "A lot of thank yous."

The nuns at the College of St. Benedict held a candlelight vigil, and the city had a ceremony to dedicate a park to Brian.

Lindgren remembered people flocking to both events. They wanted to show their support somehow. They wanted to feel a little less helpless.

One of his high school classmates owned Croat Kerfeld Homes, a building company in St. Cloud.

"He said, 'I want to do something,'" Lindgren recalled. So Lindgren started gathering donations to build Wendy and her little daughter, Katelyn, the home that Brian had been planning for them.

That helped the St. Joe police force heal. So did the community's response.

When Lindgren and his officers were out on calls, there was a different feel, an appreciation for what they did and for the stakes involved. He saw signs in the windows of random houses offering support for cops.

When a North St. Paul officer was killed in 2009, Lindgren was able to pass that comfort on. He was working in Meeker County by then, and Minnesota Public Radio asked him to weigh in on what happened to a community when an officer was killed.

"For the citizens and officers it's almost like an extended family member has died, and you have both been at the funeral together," Lindgren said. "There's that kind of a connection."

* * *

LINDGREN COMES from a long line of law enforcement. His father was a police officer, several uncles were as well, and all of his brothers, too. He has cousins who worked for the Secret Service and the Department of Homeland Security.

But by the end of his career, Lindgren wasn't sure he wanted that tradition for his children.

The St. Joe police force was tight-knit, and Brian was a key part of that.

After training sessions they would sometimes gather at Lindgren's house for pizza and beers.

"Brian would play with my kids," Lindgren said. "He was still ten years older than my oldest kid, but they'd play Nintendo."

The night Brian Klinefelter was shot, Lindgren's nine-year-old son, Justin, begged to go the hospital with his father. But Lindgren and his wife said no and left Justin with his grandma.

Twenty years later Lindgren can still remember the conversation he had with his son early the next morning.

"He said, 'Is Brian okay?' and I said 'No, he's not,'" Lindgren said.

He took a sip from his coffee cup and remembered Justin's disbelief and devastation.

"He thought that we were invincible, that bullets can't kill us," Lindgren said. "We've got vests on and that kind of stuff."

Lindgren remembered sitting on the stairs with his son as Justin broke down into sobs, struggling to find the words for how awful he felt.

"That was probably the worst," Lindgren said.

Lindgren remembered trying to explain grief to his son, trying to reassure him that the unbearable, pit-of-the-stomach despair would not last forever.

"I said it's like at the lake where you throw a rock in and it makes a big plunk," Lindgren said. "That's where we're at right now. But it will get better, and the ripples of the time going into the future will be like the ripples of water, and we're going to be okay with this."

Grasping at whatever he could to ease his son's pain, Lindgren told him that sometimes when people want to honor a fallen police officer, they displayed a blue light. He explained that the blue uniforms police officers wear represent the "thin blue line" between order and chaos. Blue is a special color, he said, and if they turned on a blue light outside, Brian would see it.

"We just found a blue Christmas bulb," Lindgren said. "It was an actual 100-watt or sixty-watt blue light bulb and I said, 'Yeah, we're gonna put that in the entryway.'"

Lindgren remembered Justin trailing him as he went out and installed the blue bulb.

"How long are we gonna leave it on?" Justin asked.

Lindgren shrugged. "Forever," he said.

"Whoa," Justin said, his eyes widening.

Lindgren remembered his son pausing and then saying very matter-of-factly, "Well, we better buy more bulbs."

Lindgren's son Josh was younger when Brian Klinefelter was shot. He didn't fully understand the sacrifice until later.

When Josh grew up, he decided to attend St. Cloud State University. He started working with campus security. Then he told his family he wanted to become a licensed police officer.

"At the time, I said, 'No, not law enforcement,'" Lindgren remembered. "Pick anything else."

Lindgren said the family even organized "an intervention" to try to talk Josh out of it.

"We've done our duty," Lindgren remembered telling his son.

"I didn't want him seeing dying bodies," he explained. "I didn't want him to hold that baby that's got its guts ripped open and is dying in your arms. I didn't want him to go through all that stuff and the night shifts and how tough it is on families and not being around for anniversaries."

Lindgren knew that Josh and Justin had grown up listening to him and his brothers sit up late telling stories about the more satisfying sides of law enforcement.

"I said to him, 'Those stories all could have turned out really bad,'" Lindgren said.

Lindgren had lost Brian Klinefelter. He had lost one of his Meeker County officers to suicide. He had uncles who worked in law enforcement lost to suicide as well. He knew the risks of the job better than most.

But Josh would not be dissuaded.

He got his law enforcement license and worked for the Carver County Sheriff's Office before returning to the St. Cloud State force, which offered him tuition remission and a promotion to lieutenant. He also worked part time for the

Foley Police Department, a small-town force just outside St. Cloud, like the one his dad used to lead in St. Joseph.

The Lindgren law enforcement line continued and despite his concerns and reservations, Brad Lindgren's pride was obvious when he talked about Josh's work.

His voice had that same warm tone when he talked about Justin, who went from playing Nintendo with Brian to working in multimedia design and graphics.

When Justin came home to his parents' house in Meeker County and turned on the track lighting his father installed in the entryway, one of the bulbs was a reassuring blue.

And the pride was there again when Lindgren showed a framed picture of his daughter, a beautiful young woman in college.

She was born two months after Brian Klinefelter died. Her name—Brianna—is in tribute to Brian and the family he left behind.

Chapter Eleven

Brian's Siblings, 1996

SARAH KLINEFELTER did not usually watch the news. Too much violence. Too much negativity.

But on January 29, 1996, she happened to flip on the television just as the evening news was starting.

Sarah was twenty-two and used to spending nights out with friends. But her dad was out of town for work, so she had come over to visit her mom. She didn't want Lois to be alone in the house.

She and her mom talked and laughed a bit when she first arrived. Her mom showed her the heart-shaped basket she'd bought to hold diapers and wipes for when Brian and Wendy brought the baby over. Then Lois started watching a movie and Sarah went upstairs to her room and turned on the television.

Sarah was about to change the channel when something the newscaster said froze her. An "officer down" near St. Joseph? Could that be right?

She switched to another channel and another newscaster was telling the same story. Police and medical personnel were responding to an officer down call in St. Joe.

Sarah ran out of the room and halfway down the stairs. "Mom, is Brian working?" she yelled.

"What?" Lois called from downstairs.

"Is Brian on duty?" Sarah called again, urgently. "There's an officer down in St. Joe. They're saying it on the news."

Lois didn't know if her son was working that night or not. She called Wendy.

Yes, Brian was on duty. Yes, he was the one who had been shot. It was bad.

Lois hung up, and she and Sarah headed for the hospital.

* * *

JASON KLINEFELTER sat in a small waiting room at the St. Cloud Hospital, hoping for word that his older brother lived.

Jason had been visiting a friend when he got a call from his fiancée, Angie, telling him Brian had been shot and he needed to get to the hospital as fast as he could.

His friend's house was just blocks away from the hospital, so Jason arrived at the ER, breathless and frantic, before any of his family members.

"My brother's a police officer. He's been shot," he had told the person behind the desk. "I need to see him."

A nurse had grabbed him by the arm and told him she would take him to a family waiting room.

"No, I need to see him," Jason had said, pulling away as she tried to steer him toward the door. "Don't sidetrack me."

Then the doors to the ER had opened and Jason saw paramedics hurry in a gurney with another prone figure on it, a young man with brown hair wearing a flannel shirt.

Eventually Jason let himself be led into the waiting room.

He sat in the room, on a padded couch, waiting for his family and word about his brother.

Jason could not imagine life without Brian. Brian was the bridge between him and Greg, the oldest Klinefelter brother. He was closer to both brothers than Jason and Greg were to each other. It had been like that as long as Jason could remember.

When they were young and the neighborhood kids gathered to play baseball or basketball, Brian was the one who made sure none of the brothers was the last person picked for a team.

When the family first moved to St. Cloud in 1985, Jason was in seventh grade, the lowest on the totem pole at Apollo High School. The first day he was eating lunch alone in the cafeteria when he looked up from his tray to see Brian strolling over to join him, and to introduce a new friend he had already made.

After the family adopted Sarah, Brian was the one who pulled her aside at recess and showed her how to make a fist and punch like a boy. Then he told her she should only use this newfound power to protect herself or a friend, and if Brian were around he would do the protecting himself.

Now the Klinefelter siblings were grown. Jason was engaged and Brian was constantly goading him to buy a house, so Brian could help him remodel it.

Jason was in the St. Cloud Police reserves, and Brian was the one who had whet his appetite for law enforcement.

Jason was a college student at St. John's University when Brian first started on the police force in town.

One summer night, Brian asked Jason to ride along with him. The college town was dead in the summertime and Jason sat in the passenger seat of Brian's squad car, wearing a t-shirt and jeans as the two cruised the mostly empty streets.

"Let's find a drunk," Jason remembered Brian saying.

He steered the car to the junction of the interstate highway and a county road. Sure enough, a man on a motorcycle swerving in and out of his lane soon came into view. He seemed to be having trouble even keeping the bike upright.

Brian hit the lights and sirens and called dispatch to let them know he would be stopping the motorcycle on suspicion of DUI.

But the instant the squad car's lights flashed, the motorcyclist took off, and the pursuit was on.

Jason remembered Brian calling out his speed: ninety, then 100, then 110, then finally 125. Construction cones on the side of the road were going by in a blur of orange. Jason's heart raced with adrenaline, and he gripped the seat under him.

At one point the motorcyclist pulled over, and Brian pulled up behind him on the shoulder. But as soon as the brothers were out of the squad car, the guy took off again.

They got back in and continued the chase. The opportunity to end the pursuit came when the motorcyclist tried to make a U-turn and the bike came out of gear. Brian pulled up behind him.

"Take him off his bike," he yelled to Jason.

Jason had the door open and was on his way out before the car even came to a full stop. He flung himself at the motorcyclist and tackled him to the ground.

At that point, he figured it was all over. But the man came up swinging.

Jason ducked away from the first punch and deployed the only fighting tactics he knew. He grabbed the collar of the man's jean jacket, pulling it over his head like a hockey player would to his opposition.

That immobilized the man's arms and Jason was able to pull him down to his knees until Brian cuffed him.

By that time backup had arrived, and they were surrounded by squad cars with flashing lights. One of them belonged to the head of security at the College of St. Benedict, who also happened to be captain of the St. Cloud Police Reserves.

"If you liked that, you ought to join the Reserves," he told Jason.

So Jason did.

He understood the risks of the job, and he knew Brian did, too. But until that night, the risks had always seemed abstract. Sitting in that waiting room, they suddenly become very real and very immediate.

A small group of people wearing scrubs walked in the door. One of them approached Jason slowly, his eyes downcast.

* * *

JASON WAS SOBBING when his mother was ushered into the room minutes later.

A nurse was there, along with an expressionless man who introduced himself as a chaplain. The chaplain faced Lois, hands folded in front of him and began to speak in a monotone. "This is always difficult . . ." he began.

Lois stopped him with a quick wave of her hand. "Cut the crap," she said. "Did he make it or not?"

"I'm sorry, no," the chaplain said.

Lois's legs crumpled under her, and she hit her head on a chair as she collapsed backwards.

Jason stood up, screamed and hurled his fist into a large framed picture hanging on the wall behind him.

The glass shattered, showering down on the couch below. Blood streamed from Jason's knuckles, but he hardly noticed.

A nurse rushed in and took in the scene with one glance. She left, but soon returned with a medical kit and began bandaging Jason's hand while he stood there, stunned and crying.

Lois had crawled over to the sofa and was picking bits of glass off of it.

"I'm sorry he did that," she said to the nurse.

The nurse looked at her and shook her head.

"Don't be," she said. "I'd have done the same damn thing."

* * *

GREG KLINEFELTER was arriving at his home in Farmington, near Minneapolis, when news stations began to pick up on the shooting of a police officer in central Minnesota.

He had gone out to get some milk. When he opened the garage door, his wife, Jen, ran out to meet him. She was hysterical, crying and shaking.

He jumped out of the car and pulled her to him, looking her over for injuries. Had she cut herself? There was no blood.

"What is it?" Greg asked. "What's wrong?"

Through sobs, Jen told him she had just seen the top story on the evening news. "A St. Joe officer was shot," she said.

Greg felt a brief jolt as the words sunk in, but his brain immediately went to work analyzing what the news might mean, or not mean.

"Listen. Okay, okay, there's a St. Joe officer that was shot," he said, placing his hands on Jen's shoulders and looking her in the eyes. "Let's play the odds here. First of all, do we even know he was working? There's eight or nine guys. Plus, okay, what if he's shot? You can get shot and have a through-and-through or whatever. I mean, you can get shot—doesn't mean he's dead. Let's just wait, you know, wait for more information."

The two went into the house, and Greg immediately got on the phone. He dialed his parents' house. No answer.

He dialed Jason's place. No answer.

Until then Greg had been calm. But he was starting to get worried. And Jen's anxiety level also rose with each unanswered call.

Then the phone rang.

"Greg?"

It was Jason.

Time slowed to a crawl. Greg knew immediately that the officer who was shot had to be Brian. And he knew before Jason even told him that Brian was dead. He could hear it in Jason's voice.

Rage, despair and helplessness hit him all at once. Greg Klinefelter let out an anguished cry and banged his fist on a closet door.

* * *

WITHIN HOURS Greg and Jen were at the hospital, hugging his mother and Jason and Sarah, everyone still in shock.

Greg was led into the operating room to see Brian's body. He was expecting a battered, bloodied corpse like something out of a war movie. But the room had been cleaned up and Brian was just lying there, almost as if he were asleep.

A white sheet covered most of his body. Only his neck and head were visible.

Everything was calm; everything was quiet. It was surreal, like Greg was seeing everything through the lens of some awful dream.

Brian was Greg's hunting and fishing buddy, the one who brought all three brothers together. Greg had watched as his little brother grew to be bigger than he was. Watched as he married Wendy and became a dad. Watched as he settled into a job he loved.

Greg rode with Brian out on patrol once. He respected what his brother did and understood, at some level, the risk involved. But he had never thought about him dying.

Greg moved to Brian's side and stroked his hair. It looked perfect. There was not a mark on him. Even the fatal bullet wound to the throat was invisible, obscured by the tracheostomy tube still in his brother's neck.

The officers out in the waiting room had told him Brian had been shot five times, but his body armor had stopped the other bullets. Greg had to see for himself.

He took a deep breath, then rolled back the sheet, exposing Brian's chest.

Greg gasped.

The bruises were so big, the centers of them so black. There were several of them, lined up in a trail leading up to Brian's neck.

God, that must have hurt like hell.

After saying a few last words to his brother, Greg turned and left the room to rejoin the rest of the family. He needed to be with them.

* * *

SARAH KLINEFELTER was in denial.

She had heard people say Brian was dead. She had walked into that room and seen his body. But she could not accept it.

He's on an island somewhere. Just chilling.

Sarah wanted to leave the hospital. She wanted to go somewhere and have a drink. Or a smoke. Anything to calm her mind. But her mother had said no way. It was frigid out. And besides, where was she going to go?

So Sarah sat out in the exterior waiting room, while Angie and Angie's mom watched her, making sure she didn't disappear.

The Klinefelters had adopted Sarah when she was two years old. The entire family welcomed her, but she had a special bond with Brian.

When she and her brothers were all young kids living in Wisconsin, they used to go play near a gully in the woods with their neighbors. The boys would get immersed in playing war or cops and robbers, but Brian never let Sarah or her neighbor friend stray far from them. He made sure they didn't get lost.

When they got older, they would tease each other, wrestle and bicker like siblings do. Brian tried to teach Sarah to drive his stick shift car one time and it did not go well. They ended up arguing, and Sarah ended up walking home.

But Brian was also caring, huggable and warm-hearted. And he always had that grin of his.

He became her counselor. She would go to him for advice on things she didn't think she could tell anyone else. Of all the people in the house, she felt Brian understood her best.

He was allowed to call her by an old nickname, "Sissy." She would not let anyone else.

When Brian became a police officer, he took her on rides in his squad car, which was exciting.

Just a few years earlier, Brian had come to her and asked her if it was okay for him to ask Wendy to marry him, and okay for Wendy to become her sister-in-law.

She had smiled at him and said, "Of course it's okay. It's more than okay."

Then she had leapt from her chair and hugged him.

That was how she wanted to remember Brian. But she and Jason and Greg would also have to reconcile the memory of him lying in that operating room.

Chapter Twelve

Brian's Siblings,
Nineteen Years Later

ALMOST TWENTY YEARS later Jason Klinefelter stood in the midst of a store full of police gear, a mural of his brother on the wall behind him. It was a picture of Brian in his police uniform, his thumbs in his utility belt and a big grin on his face. The photo circulated widely after his death.

Jason was wearing a black polo shirt and his hair was a little lighter colored, but otherwise he and the man in the mural could pass for twins. Same height, same broad shoulders, same facial features, same wide grin.

The store was called KEEPRS, one of the few retail shops in Minnesota catering specifically to law enforcement and first responders, providing uniforms, body armor, and even weapons training. It began in 1999 as a small storefront in St. Cloud. It grew to have three locations, including a new store at one of St. Cloud's busiest intersections, where Jason was working.

Full-length windows lined two of the exterior walls, and the red, white and blue sign with the KEEPRS logo outside was impossible to miss.

The mural of Brian loomed over everything inside, including a glass case with his duty belt and badge. Brian's face smiled against a background of blue sky and wispy clouds. Above his head, in large white print: "In Valor, There Is Hope."

Below stood a glass case with photos of old newspapers with headlines that told Brian's story: "St. Joe police officer killed; 1 suspect dead, 2 captured," "Klinefelter gets medal of honor," and "Klinefelter name added to memorial."

Above it, in dark print, were words from Jesus' Sermon on the Mount, Matthew 5:9. "Blessed are the peacemakers: for they shall be called children of God."

For Jason, directing sales and marketing at KEEPRS became a full-time job. But the store also gave back to the law enforcement community, solidified Jason's relationship with Greg, kept the brothers connected to Wendy and kept Brian in people's minds. It became one way Jason created something positive out of that terrible night.

* * *

THE LAST TIME Jason saw his brother alive, Jason was sitting on the floor of his parents' living room watching TV with his back up against an ottoman.

The front door opened, and Jason turned to see Brian walk in. "Hey, how's it going?" Jason said, then turned back to the television.

Brian had come over to tell his family that he had found someone who wanted to buy his green Ford Ranger. He was going to use the proceeds from the sale to make a down payment on the first house for him and Wendy and Katelyn.

By that night Brian was dead, and Jason was left to wonder what else he could have said if he had known that it was something other than just another day in his parents' living room.

Something changed inside Jason the moment he knew that his brother was dead. He was in his early twenties and, in an instant, he went from a boy to a man.

"That whole night it was like a switch flipped for me, and I felt a sense of responsibility that, to this day, I don't think I've let go of," Jason said.

Growing up, Jason had been the most happy-go-lucky of the brothers. Life was a hunting, fishing, hockey-playing romp, especially when Brian was around.

The day Brian died, Jason realized how fragile life was, and how many people around him he wanted to protect.

"You go from being the youngest with the least amount of responsibility and then sitting in a room and watching people hear the message he was killed thrusts you into a role whether you like it or not," Jason said.

By nature, Jason was outgoing and social. But after Brian's death he found himself letting fewer people into his inner circle. He found himself telling Angie he had all the friends he needed and didn't really care to know any more people.

"When you let people inside your circle, you feel an obligation to care for them," Jason said.

It can get tiring, he added. "There's only so much one person can do."

* * *

FOR SEVERAL WEEKS after Brian died, the entire St. Cloud community was talking about it.

Jason was working for Angie's father's lawn-care company. He spent much of his time driving around in the company truck, going from job to job. In those days, he was usually listening to talk radio because any sort of music could remind him of Brian and trigger an emotional reaction.

A show run by local talk radio host Emmett Keenan was becoming almost like communal therapy in St. Cloud, with people calling in every day looking for answers as to why a cop who seemingly had no enemies had been killed.

Jason stumbled across it one day. Callers were discussing why his brother had approached Kantor's truck without backup.

"They were angry," he recalled. "They were angry at Brian, like why did he walk up?"

One caller went too far.

"Brian really did a disservice to his family," the man said. "Why would he walk up to a truck without backup and do this and leave all these people behind?"

Jason pulled over and called in to the radio program, something he had not done before.

"I got on and I just said, 'You know, everything you guys are saying is stuff we've tossed around from the first day, and while it's good to ask the questions, it's not productive in resolving it,'" Jason said.

By that point, Jason said, he and his family believed that the three men in the truck had a plan, though it might not necessarily have been rational, and the end result would have been the same had Brian waited for other officers to arrive.

Someone would have died—if not Brian, then whichever officer approached the vehicle first.

"The way in which he was killed, there could have been three people around the car," Jason said. "it wouldn't have made a difference."

It was not fair to blame his brother for doing his job, Jason said. Brian had a knack for defusing tense situations and regularly went to emotional domestic disturbance calls on his own, with no backup. "Police work was just different then," Jason said.

Jason emphasized that he understood the angst the radio callers were expressing and, in fact, he appreciated how much Brian's death seemed to wrack the entire community.

He and the other Klinefelters went to a national gathering of police families a year later, and met others who had lost loved ones in the line of duty.

They talked to one family from Oakland who said their loved one's death was overshadowed by other national news, and the city quickly moved on.

In St. Cloud and St. Joseph, on the other hand, it seemed like the entire community mourned with the Klinefelters for weeks.

* * *

IN THE WAKE of Brian's death, Jason felt a responsibility to look after Wendy. At first she had plenty of support, and had plenty of things to keep her busy: the wake, the funeral, then several memorials.

But Jason wondered what would happen in the months and years after, when others moved on. How would she do then? How would the family stay connected?

At the same time, Jason and Greg were trying to navigate brotherhood without Brian. They were five years apart and Brian had been the glue between them.

"I remember having that conversation with Greg, where we looked at each other and said, 'We've got to figure this out,'" Jason said. "It's gonna be different. And it took a long time to kind of sort out."

Greg said he had to redefine his role in the family with Brian gone.

At twenty-seven, he was married and working as a market analyst in Cannon Falls, just south of the Twin Cities. It was a comfortable life, but Greg felt a void when he returned to it after Brian died.

His employer was gracious with time off, and Greg had several co-workers he felt close enough to talk to about Brian's death in detail. But it was an odd feeling. He was mourning Brian. Everything seemed to have changed. But all around him, on the job in Cannon Falls and at home in Farmington, life seemed to go on as normal, as if the world didn't know it had been shattered.

For months Greg and Jen made the two-hour drive back to St. Cloud every weekend so they could commiserate with others who truly understood the void.

"I just wanted to be back with my family," Greg said, looking back on it.

Soon, weekends were not enough.

"We moved home and, in hindsight, it was probably the best decision we made," Greg said.

The details of the transition turned hazy after almost twenty years. Greg said his mom suggested he come home and work in the family landscaping business. Lois said it was Greg's idea. Either way, it was what Greg needed.

Jason had earned his business degree, and the two of them were working in the same industry in addition to being in the police reserves together. They began to see more of each other personally and professionally and grew closer. They also began talking about selling police equipment together on the side.

The seed of the idea that would one day grow into KEEPRS was planted a few months before Brian's death, while Jason sat in the muster room at the St. Cloud Police Department with some other reserve officers.

An officer came into the room and announced that a well-known police supply company was going out of business.

"I thought, well, that's odd, they've got to be the only ones doing this," Jason said.

Jason saw a business opportunity. He had the business administration background. Greg had a degree in marketing and mass communications. Together they could form a business plan and start selling.

It was Wendy's idea to take it retail.

Two years after Brian's death, they were all in Duluth for another trial of Thomas Kantor's accomplices. The legal process was dragging on, but the upside was that all the court proceedings gathered Brian's loved ones together.

During a conversation at the hotel after a day of trial, Wendy told Jason and Greg about her idea to turn their side business into an actual storefront. She had finished her criminal justice degree but had mixed feelings about working in law enforcement.

"She wanted to stay connected to the industry, but not necessarily be *in* the industry," Jason said.

The three sat down together and started Klinefelter's Enforcement & Emergency Product, Resource, and Supply, Inc.—KEEPRS—on a yellow legal pad.

They made a list: who would get the mail, who would pay the bills, etc.

"It was so rudimentary," Jason recalled.

Dave Klinefelter monitored the budding business owners to make sure their venture strengthened rather than strained their relationships.

Lois remembers her husband time and again reminding the trio they had to maintain emotional distance between their professional lives together and their personal lives.

Dave was in the agricultural lending business. Many of his customers were sets of family members running farms together.

"I saw way too many families get split up with hard feelings," Dave said, "because they didn't know when to wear their family hats and when to wear their business hats."

But KEEPRS proved to be what the three needed. It allowed them to do something that kept Brian's memory alive, but required enough attention to detail that they could get lost in it when they needed to.

"It forced us to be together and to focus on something other than the tragedy of Brian's death," Jason said. "Because for a long time every time we got together that was all we talked about, all the time."

* * *

JASON AND GREG had figured out how to stay connected to each other. But they were both struggling to determine how close they needed to be with the law enforcement community.

Their work as reserve officers was stressful for their loved ones. Jason knew enough not to let his mother see him in his uniform, because he looked so much like Brian. He would dress in his room, with the door shut, then sneak out.

Greg was of average height and weight compared to his bigger younger brothers and did not look so much like Brian. But he was also concerned about what his mother thought every time he headed out on his reserve shifts. Still, every day he was drawn deeper and deeper into the profession and its camaraderie.

Greg remembered the rows and rows of police officers who showed up for Brian's funeral, the care and sense of family they showed for someone they never knew personally.

"I wanted to be a part of that," Greg said. "In my mind I suppose I was trying to give back."

Greg started making plans to go back to school and become a full-time police officer.

Jen was supportive. When Greg told his father, he was surprised to find Dave not only supportive, but also proud.

Soon after, with Dave behind him, Greg walked into the kitchen of his parents' house, set some books on the table and took a deep breath.

"Mom, what would you think about your oldest son becoming a police officer?" he asked.

Lois immediately started to sob.

Greg rushed around the table and hugged her.

"If you really insist, I won't do it," Greg said.

But Lois waved him off, drying her tears with the back of her hand. "Absolutely not, Greg," she said. "If that's what you want to do, you do it."

Remembering the conversation almost twenty years later, Lois said she supported her son. "It was just the shock of it," she said.

Even so, when Greg graduated from the police academy and asked his mother to pin on his badge at the ceremony, she just couldn't do it. His wife did it instead.

Greg dedicated his life to law enforcement.

"Then Jason got out of it," Lois said. "One less worry."

After Brian's death, Angie was never comfortable with Jason being a reserve officer. She made it clear that, though she loved him, and supported him, it scared her. She saw what Wendy went through and didn't think she could bear it.

With KEEPRS, Jason found what he needed: something that connected him to law enforcement without stressing his wife so much. He focused his energies on the business, helping grow it into something more than a police supply shop.

Behind one door the business had a small room with several sewing machines, where staff could do alterations to officers' uniforms on-site. Another, longer room, only slightly wider than a hallway, had a projection screen at one end.

There officers could do "shoot-or-don't-shoot" drills, playing out scenarios with a laser gun they might encounter later with a real firearm, training to make split-second decisions that could result in them or someone else not coming home.

KEEPRS is a one-stop cop shop but also an entry point for the general public to interact with law enforcement officers when they aren't enforcing the law. Anyone could walk in the door. Anyone could browse the racks.

It's a unique business model and it's been successful.

KEEPRS has made the *Inc.* 5,000 list of America's fastest growing companies multiple times.

Early on, Jason, Greg, and Wendy kept the store's connection to Brian more subtle. They were concerned about making it look like they were profiting off his death and the media attention that surrounded it.

But by the time they opened the new store in St. Cloud in 2014, they felt enough time had passed to honor him with the large mural.

Their staff numbers grew to more than twenty, and some of the new hires were only a few years old when Brian was shot. They had no firsthand knowledge of what his death meant. And they were just a fraction of the new generation growing into men and women in Central Minnesota. Jason, Greg, and Wendy wanted them to know Brian, so they made Brian a very visible part of the new store.

"It allows us to honor Brian's memory in a way we were never able to do before and we're far enough away now that we can do it without it looking like we're exploiting the tragedy," Jason said. "That was the one thing we always feared, was that people would think we were profiting off the tragedy."

* * *

THE YEARS HAVE POLISHED Brian's memory into something of a local talisman—his name placed on parks and charitable foundations and his portrait on the wall at KEEPRS.

Jason said the way Brian died put him on a pedestal, but he reveled just as much in the more intimate stories that showed his brother wasn't perfect.

He grinned when he recalled the summer days when he would take a break from the lawn care route to stop by Brian and Wendy's apartment while Brian was off work. Jason would kick off his dirty rubber boots, and the two of them would play Nintendo together for hours.

"Wendy would come home and just be livid, because there was not a dish washed, nothing picked up," Jason said, laughing.

Jason also remembered the time when Brian was on duty, watching a downed power line in St. Joseph to make sure no one touched it until utility workers came.

After about an hour he called a local pizzeria and had them deliver a pie straight to his squad car.

"He was always hungry," Jason said.

There was a glint in Jason's eyes as he told these stories, a hint of the happy-go-lucky kid he used to be—that Brian encouraged him to be.

That was still part of him, but it was balanced by the gravity of his brother's death—and what it taught him about the fragility of life.

Greg agreed it was strange to try to navigate his new relationship with Jason. It was even scary, he said. He used to envy how tight Brian and Jason were.

The two remaining brothers tried to make time for each other, even as the demands of work and family grew with the births of their children.

They live five minutes apart, Greg mused. He drove within a few blocks of Jason's house when he went to work. They should see each other more, he said. Someday, when the kids were older, he envisioned them sitting around a table in the evenings playing cards, like he used to watch his dad and his uncles do.

Greg said his favorite times were when he and Jason were out in the woods together hunting or just sitting by the river at the family's cabin. There, in the quiet of nature, they could really talk.

"I know Jason knows I love him and I care a lot about him," Greg said.

* * *

FOR SARAH KLINEFELTER the road back was rockier.

For months after Brian's death the family and Wendy would gather in the living room at the end of the day and talk about Brian. Inevitably the talk would turn to Brian's mischievous side, and there would be laughter. Sarah would leave the room then. She did not like to laugh about him. It was still too raw for her.

Sarah is now in her forties, with thick, flowing black hair and a tattoo on her left shoulder—a badge, Brian's badge, wrapped in an angel's wing, with the date 1-29-96 on it.

Sarah said she still didn't like to talk about what happened that night. She had trouble opening up and expressing her feelings. Always had. But she had kids of her own, and she wanted to set a good example for them and for her nieces and nephew.

So, in a coffee shop inside a grocery store in Sartell, she poured out her emotions, in spoken word and in handwritten notebook pages.

For a long time after Brian died, she said, she was very angry with God for letting him die. She felt lost, bitter. Sometimes she felt like she didn't want to live anymore. She wanted to be with Brian.

Every day she would ask God, "How could you? What did we do to you to deserve this? Why are you punishing us? Why wasn't I there for Brian that night?"

She felt alone, like there was no one she could talk to, even though the people who loved her kept reaching out and trying to help. She would push them away.

One friend, a woman named Jody, Sarah felt she could confide in. Jody tried to help her get back on track. Some days it worked, other days not so much.

In 2008, Sarah was still struggling with Brian's death and going through a divorce. Jody convinced her it was time to get back into church and told her to go to a place in Sartell called the Waters. "Get your butt in there," Sarah recalled Jody saying.

Since her early teen years, Sarah had felt like there was something missing in her spiritual life. She found it at the Waters. The contemporary Christian church had musicians playing electric and acoustic instruments on a stage in front of a wave-like backdrop.

But Sarah said it was the welcoming, non-judgmental atmosphere there that struck her more than the modern trappings.

The church's motto is "Love God. Love People. Love Life."

"When you walk out of that church, you just feel refreshed and clean," Sarah said. "I love it. I've finally found a place where I fit in."

The church's pastor, Doug Vagle, reminded her a little of Brian. He was laidback but had a bit of Brian's spunk. And he was there when Sarah found her faith.

One day, during the church service at the Waters, Sarah said Pastor Doug came over to her during prayer. He grabbed her hand to pray with her, and they both closed their eyes.

"All of a sudden I just felt this chill and an extra hand reaching out," Sarah said. "I swear to you, it was God. I could see part of His robe. It was Him just saying everything is going to be okay."

She pauses, reliving the moment.

"I've never felt anything like that in my life," she said.

Sarah is in a better place emotionally now. She still misses Brian, but when she wants to feel close to him she goes to the park named after him in St. Joseph or up to the family cabin on the Wisconsin border near the St. Croix State Forest.

The land was passed down from Sarah's grandfather, but the cabin was Brian's design.

While cleaning out Brian's closet in his old room, the Klinefelters found the schematic of a cabin Brian had drawn and brought it to life.

* * *

THE GOSPEL PASSAGE adorning the wall of KEEPRS is not just for show. Jason also credited faith with helping Greg and him move forward—a faith in a God who understands suffering and a God who has a plan.

"It was tested," Jason said, "and I think everybody would have their own journey they took from the time Brian died to reconcile what that meant to them."

But Jason said the question for him and his siblings was never whether Brian's death would shatter their faith entirely, but how they could make such a seemingly senseless tragedy part of their faith journey.

Greg said he drew comfort from casual conversations with an associate pastor at the family's church, a man named Jon Anderson with whom he played softball. He wondered if Anderson knew, to this day, the impact he had.

Greg and the other Klinefelters also leaned on their father and followed his example.

"My dad's an amazing person," Greg said. "He taught me a lot about forgiveness."

Greg said he now believes Brian's death was part of some greater plan, even if he does not understand it. Death comes to us all, he said, and accepting that helped him take on the risks of a career in law enforcement with some sense of peace.

"My children have some worry about my job," Greg said. "But I don't. I still think to this day, God's got a plan for us."

Greg began his career with the St. Cloud Police Department in 2006, ten years after his brother's death. He said he was doing what he was meant to do.

"I worked hard to find my niche in life," Greg said. "About a year and a half into it was when I really realized, this is what God put me on earth to do, this job. And I just felt very peaceful about it."

But it took time to get to that point.

Greg said that, on the day Brian died, he knew it was something he would not get over easily with God.

He remembered cornering his church pastor, Gerald Staehling, in the hallway of the hospital that night.

"How can this happen?" he asked the pastor. "Why does God let this happen?"

Greg said he expected some deluge of Bible verses, something that would make sense of things and make the ache in his chest subside.

But Staehling just shook his head.

"Greg, I don't know," he said. "I don't know. I don't have an answer."

Chapter Thirteen

The Pastors,
1996

As Lois Klinefelter was collapsing on the floor and Jason Klinefelter was shattering a picture in a hospital waiting room, Gerald Staehling was at a meeting at Atonement Lutheran Church.

Staehling, tall and slim with neatly combed hair turning from black to gray, had been the church's senior pastor for fourteen years—almost half his career.

He knew everyone in his congregation and enjoyed his job, even if shepherding members through tragedies sometimes drained him emotionally.

The meeting wrapped up and Staehling stood at the door, saying final goodbyes with congregants who were bundling up before walking through the frigid night to their cars.

Finally, Staehling pulled on his own coat and hat and stepped out the door, hunching his shoulders against the face-numbing wind and shoving his hands in his coat pockets. It was only a block to his house but in that weather each minute outside was miserable. He quickened his pace, ticking off sidewalk tiles with long strides.

Few cars were on the road to his right. A solitary ambulance screamed by, sirens wailing. That was not unusual. The street was a main thoroughfare in north St. Cloud and it led straight to the hospital. Staehling had heard sirens during the church meeting as well.

He hopped up the front steps of his house and burst in the door, shutting it quickly behind him and shaking off the cold.

"Woo," he said to his wife. "It's freezing out there."

Staehling barely had his coat off and hung in the closet when the phone rang.

The words that came through the receiver made his heart ache. He gripped the kitchen counter to steady himself. It was the hospital chaplain. Brian Klinefelter had been shot while on duty. The doctors could not save him. His family members were at the hospital, and they were distraught.

Staehling hung up the phone and went back to the closet to get his coat.

* * *

ON THE SHORT DRIVE to the hospital, Staehling tried to wrap his brain around the idea that Brian Klinefelter was dead.

It didn't seem possible. Just a few weeks earlier he had presided at the baptism of Brian's daughter, Katelyn. A perfect little baby, with a beautiful mother and a proud father with that huge grin.

Staehling knew the Klinefelters well. They had moved to St. Cloud a few years after Staehling became pastor of Atonement, and they soon became enmeshed in the church life.

They attended services regularly and put their kids in Sunday school and confirmation classes. Dave led Bible studies and took leadership positions. They were one of Atonement's rock-solid families.

Greg was in high school when the Klinefelters first joined the church. Brian was in junior high. Staehling had kids the same age who became friends with the older Klinefelters and played side-by-side with them on the Apollo football team.

Brian was a good kid—helpful, obedient. But he had a mischievous side that Staehling got to know as well.

Staehling was also a chaperone on the Colorado trip when Brian snuck off to watch the Broncos game.

That mild roguish side to Brian always remained, but Staehling watched it tempered by maturity as he grew up.

Staehling had taught Brian's confirmation class and Brian took it seriously, asking and answering difficult questions about his faith. Staehling was the presider when Brian married Wendy at a young age, casting off the single life for the promise of "'til death do us part." Staehling congratulated Brian when he got his first job as a full-time police officer and saw the excitement in his eyes. Staehling sat Brian and Wendy down before Katelyn's baptism and talked to them not only about their faith, but also about the risks involved with being a police family. He saw resolve in Brian's eyes then, as Brian told Staehling he understood the risks but felt he was well-trained and believed strongly that police work was what he was meant to do.

Staehling had felt pride at the transformation. The boy he had known was budding into manhood—as a police officer, as a husband, and as a father.

And now he was dead.

Staehling tightened his grip on the steering wheel and choked back tears as he pulled the car into the hospital parking lot.

* * *

THE EMERGENCY ROOM was packed with police officers. Staehling had expected a lot of them, judging by the number of squad cars in the parking lot, but he was still shocked by the sea of blue humanity he had to wade through to get to the nurse's desk.

The officers were standing around, shuffling their feet, sniffing back tears, some looking at the floor, some hugging each other. Staehling had seen a lot of sorrow in his job. This would match it all. He took a deep breath as he introduced himself and told the nurse he had been sent for.

Staehling was ushered into an ER surgical room, white-walled and full of beeping, blinking machines. Brian's tall, broad body was laid out on a stretcher in the middle of the room, covered by a sheet up to his bare neck and shoulders.

This was where they had tried to save him.

A few doctors and nurses still remained, in light blue scrubs and blood-spattered surgical gowns. They said little, except to tell Staehling they had done everything they could. Their faces were obscured by goggles and paper masks, but their disappointment and frustration was palpable.

Staehling gathered the family members already at the hospital. At that point they still waited on Greg, who was coming up from the Cities, and Dave, who was at a conference in Fargo.

Jason was distraught, his hand bleeding and bandaged. Lois was weeping. Sarah just seemed stunned.

Staehling led them in a short, emotional prayer service. He could say nothing except beg for God to speed Brian to his side and speed comfort to those he left behind.

Then Staehling went out into another room filling up with Brian's closest friends and extended family and talked to them and led them in prayer. He felt an avalanche of grief. There were long, sobbing hugs and tears pouring down cheeks.

Staehling was there for hours as one by one, Brian's loved ones cried themselves to exhaustion and began to leave for home because there was nothing left to do.

In tearful conversations, he pieced together what had happened. Three young men had robbed a liquor store in Albany of a few hundred dollars. When Brian stopped their truck in St. Joe, one of them shot him with no warning, and they left him bleeding on the side of the road.

The three split up, and the one who killed Brian was stopped in Sauk Rapids and shot dead after a standoff. The other two surrendered without a fight.

Sometime after midnight, when almost everyone had gone home and the hospital was eerily quiet, the hospital chaplain found Staehling and took him to see the body of the man who shot Brian.

They rode an elevator down to the bowels of the hospital, to the dark, quiet morgue where Thomas Kantor lay spread out on an examination table.

Brian's body was a few floors up, his life full of promise cut short. His killer lay cold and lifeless on this sterile metal table, a bullet hole in his chest—another young man dead, with no hope of justice for the Klinefelters and no chance to ask him "why?" Staehling saw him as another young man who should have had many years ahead of him to try and make a positive mark on the world. Instead he'd thrown those years away in a spasm of violence.

As Staehling stared down at the body, no Biblical phrases sprang to his head to comfort him.

All he could think was one thing.

What a waste.

* * *

ATONEMENT'S ASSOCIATE PASTOR, Jon Anderson, didn't find out about Brian Klinefelter's death until the next morning.

Anderson, a young minister with tightly curled brown hair, had come to Atonement about five years earlier after a stint at a Houston church. He had been through several tragedies there, but the news about Brian still hit him hard. Like Staehling, he was close with the Klinefelters. He had played softball with Brian regularly. Dave had helped him teach confirmation classes. He had been there for Katelyn's baptism.

Immediately that morning, Anderson and Staehling faced two challenges: planning what would certainly be a high-profile funeral and serving as counselors for a congregation traumatized by violence.

It wasn't just the Klinefelters, after all.

Doug Thomsen and his family also went to Atonement. Anderson went to visit Doug after learning about his role in the night's events. He found him happy to be alive, but still visibly shaken. The memories of what happened were vivid: Kantor barging into his bedroom, driving with the gun on him, the darkness of the trunk, the single gunshot. It was clear that Doug would relive the details for years to come.

Roger Anhorn, the state police officer who helped inspire Brian to go into law enforcement, was also a member of Atonement. He was despondent and guilt-ridden.

The number of people from Atonement directly affected by the night of mayhem defied explanation. It seemed like more than one congregation should have to bear.

Anderson knew from past experience that communities in shock and mourning sometimes seem to fishtail like a car that's lost traction—jerking from one emotional response to another, overcorrecting as they tried to make sense of the tragedy.

Staehling knew that, as the presider at the funeral, people would look to him to make some sense of the senseless.

His personal inclination was to talk about the proliferation of guns in society, including the handgun Kantor used to kill Brian. But he knew that, for the Klinefelters, that was not an issue. They owned guns, they hunted. When Staehling had talked to Dave Klinefelter about gun control in the past, Dave had used the familiar phrase "Guns don't kill people. People kill people."

So Staehling continued to contemplate what to say at a funeral that was going to be bigger than any he had been a part of before.

Police groups from across the state were phoning in their intention to attend and looking for details. News about the shooting was on the front page of the St. Cloud paper every day and it seemed like the entire city was talking about it. Some residents with no connection to law enforcement or the Klinefelters would certainly come. Hundreds of St. Joseph residents were also likely to attend.

It became obvious quite quickly that Atonement would not be able to accommodate the crowd. Wendy was Catholic. When she married Brian, Staehling had presided alongside a priest. But Wendy's parish in St. Joseph wasn't big enough, either.

That was when the nuns at St. Benedict's Monastery in St. Joseph stepped forward.

The sisters were affiliated with a 2,000-student all-girls college, the College of St. Benedict, that had recently built a fieldhouse with room for thousands. They offered the space to Staehling and assured him that in a few days they could make it appropriate for a funeral.

An ecumenical effort to accommodate the throngs began. A group of women at Atonement who prepared lunches for post-funeral receptions joined with a similar group from St. Benedict and scaled up their meal preparations.

A stage was set up at the front of the fieldhouse, with an altar and pots and pots of flowers. Hundreds of folding chairs were brought in and set up in neat rows facing the stage.

A space was left in between the altar and the chairs. That was where Brian's casket would go.

Staehling and Anderson were also planning a visitation for the Klinefelters the night before the funeral. When Anderson went to their house, he saw it filling up with flowers and food from people who didn't know how else to express their sympathy.

Hot dishes filled the family freezer and more sat in coolers out on the deck, where the temperature was even lower.

Staehling was busy with funeral arrangements but had a couple meetings with the family. He had served as an Army chaplain and dealt with deadly helicopter crashes and other tragedies.

He could tell the Klinefelters were still somewhat in shock, but also beginning the grieving process. Staehling wanted to grieve with them, but he knew from experience he had to put some emotional distance between himself and the work he needed to do arranging a funeral and preaching the gospel messages of forgiveness and the promise of salvation.

Dave and Jason agreed to give the eulogy. Greg was going to make some closing comments. Lois, Sarah, and Wendy preferred to stay in the background, but were clear on what they did not want.

Staffers for the governor and a U.S. senator had called and said their bosses wanted to speak at the funeral.

"Absolutely not," Lois said.

"This is not a circus," Greg added. "We need to have this right."

Dave had a song he wanted played at the funeral, a Catholic hymn Brian had heard at Wendy's church and really liked. Staehling had never heard it before, but he listened to it in between meetings and agreed it was perfect for the service.

As one of the meetings was wrapping up, Staehling gave the Klinefelters a bit of advice he had given probably dozens of times before: give everyone space to grieve in their own way.

There was no single right way for a person to express sorrow, Staehling said. Lois collapsing on the floor was okay. Jason smashing a picture with his bare hand was okay. So was Dave's relative stoicism.

They needed to grieve in their own ways, but they also needed to let the community mourn with them.

Hundreds showed up for the visitation the night before the funeral. The receiving line snaked around the wall of the field-house. One by one, each person offered Wendy and the Klinefelters tearful hugs.

By the time it was over, Staehling could tell they were exhausted, mentally, physically and spiritually. And they hadn't even been through the funeral.

* * *

THE DAY BRIAN Klinefelter was laid to rest was again frigid— negative twenty-six degrees.

Hotels serving the many funeral-goers provided free jump starts for cars left out in cold parking lots. A local RV dealer offered its heated car wash bay free to any of the hundreds of police vehicles descending on Clemens Fieldhouse on the College of St. Benedict campus.

Staehling watched the officers file in, two-by-two, and take their seats in the folding chairs. They streamed in wearing their service parkas—wave after wave of police navy blue, county sheriff brown and state trooper maroon. They just kept coming.

After the chairs were all occupied, officers took places along the walls, two deep, on the running track that surrounded the fieldhouse. Each of them was somber and silent, their hands clasped in front of them, facing the stage.

Jason had gotten a look at the fieldhouse the night before and had registered the family's approval. The sisters at St. Benedict's Monastery and the volunteers from Atonement had made good on their promise to turn the gym into a church.

On the stage everything was white. The altar was white, surrounded by white flowers. Brian's casket was draped in white, flanked by a pair of officers in dress uniforms with ceremonial rifles slung over their shoulders.

More officers streamed in, looking for places to stand.

The St. Joseph force was the last to come in, led by Chief Lindgren in his dress whites. The rest came in behind him, single file, four in dark blue, four in light blue. They were escorted to the front row on the right side of the rows of chairs.

Anderson was on the stage, behind a podium. Staehling was preparing to lead in the processional, including two acolytes with the cross and Bible. The Klinefelters would enter behind them.

Everyone in the crowd stood for a color guard—three officers walking in lockstep carrying the American flag, the Minnesota state flag, and a white flag dedicated to police officers.

"Peace be with you," Anderson said after the flag ceremony was over.

Anderson, dressed in a white cassock, then adjusted his wire-rim glasses and read from a prayer book open in front of him.

"'He comforts us in all our sorrows so that we can comfort others in their sorrows with the consolation we ourselves have received from God,'" he said.

"'As Christ was raised from the dead, by the glory of the father we too might live a new life.

"'If we were united with him in a death like his, we shall certainly be united with him in a resurrection like his.'"

A group of musicians to the right of the stage began to play. The song was based on the Beatitudes, words from Jesus' Sermon on the Mount.

"'Blessed are they, full of sorrow,'" the choir sang. "'They shall be consoled.'"

The song was Staehling's cue, and he began to lead the procession into the fieldhouse. The acolyte bearing the cross came in first, then Staehling. The Klinefelters walked behind him, Wendy leaning on Dave and Lois for support. When they reached Brian's casket, the family split off and went to the front row of chairs on the left side, while Staehling continued on to the altar.

Staehling gazed on the banner behind the altar with the words "MAKING CHRIST KNOWN" on it in large black print. That was his job. To make Christ known in the midst of this sorrow.

Then he turned to face the crowd and began the service.

"Oh, God of grace and glory, we remember before you today our brother Brian," Staehling said. "We thank you for giving him to us to know and love as a companion. Console us who mourn. Give us your aid so that we might see in death the gate to eternal life."

The fieldhouse was silent as Timothy Haeg, a longtime friend of Brian, began the first reading, a well-known Bible passage from Ecclesiastes that inspired the folk song "Turn! Turn! Turn! (To Everything There Is a Season)."

"Everything that happens in this world happens at the time God chooses," Haeg said. "He sets the time for birth and the time for death."

After Haeg finished, a choir of nuns from St. Benedict began to sing. It was an old song, about the martyrs and a choir of angels greeting the deceased in heaven. A song about everlasting rest. The song had been sung by people of faith for centuries for those who have died.

Their voices soared in practiced, perfect unison, and hardened police officers wiped tears from their eyes.

Darryl Eiynck, another friend of Brian, gave the second reading, a passage from the end of the Gospel of John in which Jesus tells his followers not to be worried or upset.

"'There are many rooms in my father's house,'" Eiynck read. "'And I am going to prepare a place for you.'"

The nuns sang again, this time in Latin, and the strains of the ancient language filled the fieldhouse, echoing off the walls.

Then Dave and Jason walked up to the podium to give the eulogy. Jason's boyish face looked young for the suit he was wearing, but his tall, broad frame filled it. He wiped his nose with a tissue as he walked up to the altar behind his father.

Dave began by telling the audience about Brian's first five days, which he spend in a neonatal intensive care unit, fighting to breathe and live.

"We had close to twenty-six years, wonderful years, with Brian that we will cherish because we could have very easily not had him at all," Dave said. "For this opportunity we are deeply grateful to God."

Dave said that Brian was destined to become a police officer, that he would make siren noises while pushing his matchbox cars around the floor and "handcuff anything he could get his hands on, especially his unsuspecting siblings."

Dave's voice was strong and steady.

Brian had achieved his dream job, and he had built a family better than he had dreamed of, Dave said.

"Just last Monday when Brian dropped off Katelyn, he told Lois how he loved Katelyn and Wendy and didn't know how he would be able to live without them," Dave said.

In the front row, Wendy broke down. Her head dropped, and her hands covered her face.

For just a moment, Dave faltered. His voice cracked. He took a deep breath and gathered himself.

"This could be a moment when hate could replace love," Dave said. "Especially when we think of those who did this to Brian. To do so would not be thinking as Brian did. Let all of us stay at his level. He would be concerned about the real causes that create violence and crime. Then devote all his efforts to try and correct them."

Dave finished and turned to give way to Jason, who touched his father on the shoulder and arm as they traded places.

The younger Klinefelter began by talking about Brian's generosity and his protectiveness when it came to his siblings.

Staehling was still reflecting on Dave's words. There was an incredible grace to them, a gentle wisdom in his commitment to turning away from hate and toward love in the name of the son he had lost.

If they could truly live that out, the Klinefelters would be okay. If everyone could love like that, the world would be okay.

Jason paused briefly while talking about the first time everyone got together to play cards after Katelyn was born. Brian kept interrupting the game to get up and check on the baby, even though he knew she was fine.

"He just liked to look at her, to love her, to smell that new baby smell and to give her kisses to let her know how much he loved her," Jason said.

He paused, inhaled deeply, then looked right at the casket below him.

"We love you, Brian," Jason said. "We'll miss you, Brian. Thank you, Brian."

Then it was Staehling's turn.

First he gave the gospel reading, another passage from John.

"'The word was the source of life and this life brought light to the people,'" Staehling said. "'A light shines in the darkness and the darkness has never put it out.'"

Then he started his sermon, telling the story of Brian growing from a mischievous boy who escaped a Christian conference to watch a football game, to a devoted officer, husband, and father.

"I, like the rest of you, have been deeply wounded—deeply wounded and angered by the events of this past week," Staehling said. "So what do we say to this? Obviously, first we turn to God's word, and in that word we hear that a light shines in the darkness and the darkness does not put it out."

Staehling looked out at the sea of police officers as he said that Brian deeply loved his job, that he believed in the thin blue line between order and chaos, that he wanted to be part of it and the best of what it stood for: to protect the vulnerable, to serve all. Brian loved his life, Staehling said, and loved God.

"The tragedy here today is that not all the forces in our world love life the way Brian loved life," Staehling said. "There are forces of darkness in our community that cheapen life, take it away from those who love life. It was against these very forces, these forces of darkness, that Brian was ready and willing as a police officer to put his life on the line."

Staehling talked about the conversation he had with Brian and Wendy before Katelyn's baptism, about how Brian knew the risks of the work he was doing, but did it anyway because he wanted to be a point of light in the world. He wanted to be part of the light God promises the darkness will not overcome.

"I have to be honest with you today," Staehling said. "There are times when our faith is tested. Yes, even as a pastor, there are times when my faith is tested. There are times when God seems so distant, and it seems that these senseless deaths don't have to happen, and why is it that they happen so frequently?"

Staehling paused. He looked out over the crowd: Brian's family and friends seated in rows to his left, the police officers sitting across the aisle and standing throughout the building.

"I'm tempted to use this moment to speak bitterly about the growing violence in our society and how we need to turn the corner on this issue of gun control, especially handguns and violence in all forms in our culture," Staehling said. "Then I remember . . . then I remember that the nature of our world is that it is a risky place. As Christians we deal with the good, and we deal with the bad. And for the most part we learn to live by grace, don't we? Each day trusting in God's love and trusting in God's goodness. I would encourage Brian's family to fall back into God's grace today. Although it may feel strange and you may not feel it, to trust in God's goodness."

This was the conclusion Staehling had come to. That Brian's death could not be an ending to his story, but rather another chapter. That the ending was yet to be written, and would be written by what his family and the community did in his name. It could not be just a waste. Some good had to come of this.

"We give thanks to God for Brian's life among us," Staehling said. "We also give thanks for the resurrection victory that belongs to Brian through Jesus Christ, and as we leave here today I think it would be helpful if all of us would pledge to work in our own community and in our own way to make this world a safer and a better place to live."

He paused, then repeated himself. "A safer and a better place to live. Then I think Brian would be happy. I think Brian would want us to do that because that is what he had dedicated his life to doing. Amen."

Staehling stepped away from the podium, and the hymn that Brian had loved began to play.

> *Do not be afraid, I am with you.*
> *I have called you each by name.*
> *Come and follow me.*
> *I will bring you home.*
> *I love you and you are mine.*

Chapter Fourteen

The Pastors,
Nineteen Years Later

J ON ANDERSON became a bishop. He has been for more than a decade.

Anderson left Atonement for a job at a church in southern Minnesota just a few months after Brian Klinefelter was killed.

But he never forgot the funeral or hearing Dave Klinefelter urge the audience to move forward and not carry a grudge against those who killed his son.

"I remember it was not what I'd expected he was going to say," Anderson said. "I was thinking at the time that the family would have to literally practice forgiveness day after day for the rest of their lives because I don't think you ever get over the loss and the destruction of a child or a spouse or a parent. That's something you carry the rest of your life.

"So that pronouncement of forgiveness was stunning."

And while Dave may not have explicitly said the words, "I forgive them," at the funeral, he did say them to Gerald Staehling, and it made a similar impact on him.

"I remember the day when Dave told me, 'You know, I've forgiven those guys,'" Staehling said.

Staehling has been retired since 2006. But the night of Brian's death and the day of his funeral remain vivid to him as well.

For the two pastors—one seasoned and one relatively green—the death of Brian Klinefelter was a test of their faith.

And the witness shown by the Klinefelters helped them—and their congregation—pass that test.

Staehling called it "a great witness to their faith and the ability to forgive."

He added, "They could have spent the rest of their lives being bitter, you know. And they haven't."

Staehling knew that to be true because he worked alongside Dave and the others in the years that followed to try to strengthen Central Minnesota families in the hopes that family ties would keep young people from slipping into crime and violence.

It went back to those three men, Staehling says: Thomas Kantor, Kenneth Roering Jr., and Brian Ederhoff. How did they get so sidetracked in life that they would do the things they did that night?

"We see that on TV every day, don't we?" Staehling said. "It's still out there. It's not going away."

The challenge for people of faith, Staehling said, is to keep up hope that a better world is possible. So his message at the funeral was not centered so much on explaining why such a dark thing as Brian's death occurred, but rather what those gathered could do to ensure such darkness didn't overshadow the light.

"Our world is so imperfect that people do these things to each other," Staehling said. "And we have to look at the fact that, in our world, we have to try to be a voice for good, and somehow or other out of all of this, there has to be some good that comes."

The good began almost immediately after Brian died, the two pastors said, and it came from how the church and the community at large responded to his death.

The way the Benedictine sisters, in particular, welcomed the entire city, regardless of creed, to come and mourn with them was striking to Anderson.

"There was amazing generosity and care shown by the sisters," Anderson said. "It was one of the deeper and more beautiful ecumenical experiences of my life. And I've had many."

Staehling watched the Atonement congregation move on in the years that followed Brian's death and saw a community changed. The shared tragedy brought a close group even closer.

"So many people came forward to reach out to the Klinefelters," Staehling said. "If you asked them if they had a part in the Klinefelter event, they would probably say, 'Yes. This is what I did.' They carry that with them for the rest of their lives."

But congregations change. Families come and go, people die, pastors retire. Staehling said that perhaps now at Atonement not everyone knows the story of what happened the night Brian Klinefelter was killed, or what happened afterward. But it's worth telling, he said.

Staehling said he learned a lot about the power of forgiveness, not only from the Klinefelters, but also from Doug Thomsen.

"I think that in forgiving a harm done to you you're not necessarily letting the other person off the hook, but you are letting yourself move beyond it and not letting it destroy your life," Staehling said. "I think that's what forgiveness does. It's the Christian model: love one another as God loves us, and when somebody does you a harm, move beyond it."

Staehling said he has told and retold the stories of Doug and the Klinefelters to others, using it as a model of forgiveness for those who desperately need it.

"I have had lots of people in my office over the years who have been literally destroyed in life because they can't forgive," Staehling said.

That could have happened to several communities the day Brian died, Staehling said. He remembered being out at the windswept cemetery after the funeral, in the most frigid air imaginable, and feeling like all of his congregation, all the city of St. Joseph, and all the police officers in Minnesota were in mourning.

Anderson felt the same. To this day, the sound of bagpipes brings him back to that ceremony.

"Through my career, I hope I never ever have to preside at the funeral of a police officer again," Anderson said. "That was so, so sad in so many ways."

That sense of community shock, of disruption of social order and feelings of loss even among those not related to Brian became part of Anderson's teachings about violence and the sin of criminal acts.

"When I would subsequently teach about the fifth commandment and God's command to not kill, I would often come to talk about this," Anderson said, "because I think we think about the impact of our decisions in such individualistic terms but actually all acts of violence like this tear at the social fabric and damage the community and the sense of safety and trust."

Brian's death was a reminder, Anderson said, that bad things happen to all people, even good people. That difficult truth was driven home by how widely beloved he was.

Anderson remembered Sarah talking about what Brian meant to her and finishing with, "He was my brother, too."

"And I remember at the time thinking, 'Yeah that's true for all of us,'" Anderson said. "Brian was our brother."

The Klinefelter family's graceful response to the tragedy became the whole community's response. Their forgiveness was a gift that is still giving.

Years after Anderson left Atonement, his son, while walking in Minneapolis, was the victim of a hit-and-run accident that badly injured his back.

The driver who hit him was never caught, and Anderson said he harbored anger for a long time at this unknown person who was so callous with his child's life to leave him there on the pavement.

But Anderson knew he had to forgive, and that was when he realized just how hard a task that had to have been for the Klinefelters.

"Their son had been taken from them," Anderson said. "So I think their courageous decision to move forward and practice forgiveness—as painful and as difficult as that was—helped the community to move forward. Communities can go to war on each other when they get disappointed. Families can go to war in the middle of funerals. In that brokenness, we can take it out on each other. In this case, the Klinefelters continued to be the beautiful people I had known them to be."

The funeral was what most people saw of the Klinefelters' journey to forgiveness. But it was only the beginning.

Chapter Fifteen

Dave Klinefelter, 1996

DAVE KLINEFELTER was at a Holiday Inn in Fargo when he got the hardest phone call his wife ever had to make. Lois told him through tears that she and Jason were at the hospital. Brian had been shot. The doctors had tried to save him but Brian didn't make it.

Dave sat on the bed in his empty hotel room, stunned, holding the receiver up to his ear as the winter wind howled outside the window. He had just spoken to Brian that morning, before he left for the conference. Brian had stopped by the house to let him know he had sold his truck.

Now Brian was dead?

Dave needed to get home.

"Don't you dare drive home alone." Lois worried not only about the bitter cold and icy roads, but Dave's emotional state.

But Dave was not going to wait for someone to give him a ride. He mechanically went through the motions of repacking his bag, his mind still occupied with trying to process the idea of Brian being gone.

What happened? Who were these people who shot him? What had they done that led them into Brian's path?

He told the two people working the reception desk that he needed to check out before even spending one night. His son had been shot.

"What's the bill?" he asked.

One of the clerks shook her head. "There's no bill," she said. "You need to get going."

Dave hurried out into the cold to his car. He unlocked the doors and swung his bag into the passenger seat, then climbed in the driver's side and slammed the door shut.

He had been outside for less than thirty seconds, but his fingers were already a bit numb. He rubbed his hands together a few times before trying to insert the key in the ignition.

Thankfully, the Ford Taurus started.

Snow was piled in banks along both sides of Interstate 94 and blowing hard across the road. Dave had two fears. One was that the highway would be closed at some point. The other was that visibility would be too low for him to proceed even if it was open.

But just as he pulled onto the mostly deserted highway, a semi truck went by.

Dave pulled the car up behind the semi at a reasonable distance. He matched the truck's speed and locked in the cruise control, allowing the high, wide trailer to block the wind and blowing snow. The road was mostly dry.

Only then, with his car hurtling down I-94 toward his family, was Dave able to really think about Brian's death.

It didn't seem real.

Am I dreaming? I must be dreaming. This can't be true.

Dave kept hoping he would wake up. But the back of the semi remained in front of him, his fingers remained curled around the steering wheel, and soft music from the radio continued to play.

As the reality began to sink in, anger welled up inside him.

What in the world is going on? Why did God let this happen? And, Brian, why in the world did you walk up to that truck and get shot?

Dave raised his hand and smacked the steering wheel.

Slowly the anger dissipated and was replaced by a deep, aching sadness that felt like a hole opening up in his stomach.

Dave started to cry. He wiped his eye with the back of his hand, then quickly grabbed the wheel again.

I can't break down here. I'm on the freeway, doing seventy behind a semi. I've got to keep it together. I've got to get home safe.

In the depths of his despair, Dave remembered when Brian was first born. He was premature and there were complications. Dave remembered watching his tiny son cling to life in the neonatal intensive care unit and praying over and over again that God would give him more time.

He had gotten twenty-six years.

Why couldn't you give me more than twenty-six years?

Then Dave remembered the desperation of those first days, when he would have gladly accepted the promise of that much time. His faith kicked in.

Oh, man, but I did get twenty-six years.

That emotional cycle repeated itself, again and again, until Dave arrived at the hospital three hours later.

* * *

THE CHRISTIAN FAITH that led Dave Klinefelter to give the eulogy that set a tone of forgiveness a week later was fostered on a dairy farm in Marine on St. Croix, a tiny town on the Minnesota-Wisconsin border just northeast of the Twin Cities.

Dave grew up there with his mother, father, three brothers, a sister, and his grandmother. It was a close-knit family, with the Lutheran Church at the center of it.

For as long as Dave could remember, there was no question about whether they would go to church each week. They would go, as sure as the sun would rise and the cows would need to be milked each day.

He and his brothers helped with the milking, and then the family would eat together, two meals a day, breakfast and dinner, and talk to each other.

Dave went to Sunday school, and his parents and grandma reinforced the lessons he learned there with gentle course corrections when he got off track.

His mother doled out discipline to all three boys equally, telling them that she didn't want to spend her time figuring out who was at fault, so they needn't bother tattling on each other. If one of them got in trouble, they all would. So the brothers learned to stay mum about their fights, even when one of them returned to the house bloodied.

Dave's mother was also his 4-H leader.

When he was twelve and showing Jersey heifers at a local county fair, he met another 4-H member, a younger girl named Lois, who was also showing Jersey heifers.

She and her family lived in nearby Forest Lake and were also Lutherans. In Lois's case, it was usually her mother who took the family to church on Sundays. Her father, though he backed his wife, was a farmer who felt closer to God when he was out working the land. He only went on special occasions.

The year after they met, Dave went through confirmation at his church, accepting the Lutheran religion of his own free will.

Then he spent years in "Luther League," a group of young Lutherans who gathered regularly for food, Bible study, and activities. Sometimes, at big events where several Luther Leagues from across the area gathered, he would see Lois, who by then had become his friend.

Both were shy, but they became each other's regular dates when one needed a companion for school dances or other socials.

They started going out more regularly. His grandma would watch out the window and if Dave forgot to open the car door for Lois, she would gently remind him the next morning.

After high school Dave spent a few years in the U.S. Army, hopping from base to base in southeast Asia. Then he returned to the States and finished college in River Falls, just across the Wisconsin border from his hometown. He and Lois remained close. After he graduated, he made her his wife.

One of their wedding gifts was a one-year book of devotional prayers given to them by a pastor. They brought it with them on their honeymoon in St. Charles, Illinois, and read to each other every morning.

The devotionals continued every day for the first year of their marriage.

Before long, they had their own family to bring up in the church. Greg came first and then Brian. Brian was born slightly premature and had hyaline-membrane disease, a respiratory ailment that had him spending the first week of his life in the neonatal intensive care unit, struggling to breathe.

Dave and Lois prayed their tiny son would survive, that they would get the time to raise him and to know his personality. And when they got to bring him home a few weeks later, they believed their prayers had been answered.

Jason came later, and the Klinefelters completed their family by adopting a girl, Sarah.

They took the kids to church each week and to Sunday school, they participated in Bible studies, were active in their congregation and watched as their children grew up healthy, happy and well-adjusted.

The foundation of faith they had built over the years was strong enough to endure the quake of Brian's death.

But that did not make enduring it easy.

When the initial shock wore off, the family missed many things about Brian right from the start.

Dave remembered how every time Brian would come over to the house, his burly son would immediately wrap him up from behind in a bear hug and lift him off his feet.

Then he would set Dave down and say, with that big Brian smile, "So what are you doing today?"

When Dave thought about those Brian hugs, and then realized he would never get another, it was hard not to cry.

In those initial days and weeks, Lois was often more introspective. She needed more time to process her emotions.

But sometimes the script flipped.

One day she and Dave were driving together down Highway 15 in St. Cloud, near where KEEPRS would one day be, when suddenly Dave lost it.

"Why did it have to be Brian?" he said, his voice cracking.

Lois turned to him from the passenger seat. "Well, who would you have preferred it to happen to?" she said calmly.

Years later, Dave would still remember how those words echoed in his head.

Who would you have preferred it to happen to?

No one.

Nothing good had happened that night for anyone. Two young men were dead, and two others were heading to prison. Dozens more were traumatized by violence and loss.

That could not be the end of the story. But what could be done to create something good out of it?

* * *

IN THOSE FIRST few weeks after Brian's death, the Klinefelters were overwhelmed by the generosity of people who wanted to do something—anything—for them.

Neighbors and friends came, one after another, bearing plastic containers of food. Soon the refrigerator and seven coolers out on the snow-covered back porch were full.

The living room was a jungle of plants, each one accompanied by a condolence card. There was one slim path to walk through, a tunnel surrounded by flowers. More flower delivery trucks pulled into their driveway daily.

The mailbox was packed full of cards every day, and every night Dave and Lois, the kids, and Wendy sat down and opened them together.

One day there were simply too many cards to stuff in the box. The mailman brought the overflow to the door and hand-delivered them.

"I'm so sorry," he said to Lois, tears streaming down his face.

Another day the doorbell rang and it was a six-year-old neighbor boy.

The boy said he wanted to talk to Dave. Dave sat down with him, and the boy pressed a small, multi-colored agate with jagged edges into his hand.

"It's my very favorite," the boy said. "But I want you to have it for Brian."

Dave, the rock of his family, broke down sobbing at the boy's kindness.

Days later another neighbor, this one a grown man, came to the door and confessed he had intended to come over five times before and couldn't bring himself to do it.

"I just didn't know what to say," he said.

"That's okay," Dave said, patting his shoulder. "There's nothing anyone can say. But we appreciate you coming over."

The Klinefelters were amazed at how many lives Brian had touched and how much people were affected by his death. The goodwill that was pouring out to them was so powerful, Dave wanted to channel it into something.

* * *

IN THE DAYS following the funeral, Dave thought a lot about the last conversation he and his son had. Brian had sold his truck, and he had been excited to tell his dad the news. That was it. Pretty ordinary. But Dave knew he would never forget it. The last time he talked to Brian.

On the first day he returned to work after the funeral, Dave pulled out of his driveway and turned onto the road behind a green truck that looked just like Brian's.

It was odd. There just weren't too many pickups in that particular color. Then he glanced up in the rearview mirror and saw another green truck behind him.

The two trucks, one ahead and one behind followed him all the way to his office, as if escorting him back to work.

Dave parked, then watched as the two trucks moved out of sight. It felt like divine intervention, a sign. Some good would come out of this. He just had to figure out how to make it happen.

Dave settled into his chair and turned on his computer. He was the CEO of an agriculture lending firm, but his office was not particularly large.

He had the usual fabric-covered chairs and the wood desk with pictures of his family on it. Having a picture of Brian's big smile at work that he could look at whenever he wanted was reassuring.

After Dave had listened to some phone messages and gone through a stack of new papers on his desk, Marv Siekman, a financial consultant with the firm, appeared in the doorway.

Marv was about forty, a husband, and father of three young kids whose family went to the same church as the Klinefelters. He had red hair and an ever-present smile.

"C'mon in, Marv," Dave said.

Marv had a few work-related items he wanted to go over. After he and Dave had discussed those, Marv lingered on the other side of the desk, fingering some papers nervously.

"It's good to have you back, Dave," Marv said.

He was still smiling, but Dave sensed something was hanging in the air between them. "Would you like to talk about Brian?" he asked.

Marv turned serious, nodding.

"I'd love to," Marv said. "I . . . I mean . . . if that's okay."

Dave nodded and smiled, motioning to one of the chairs on the other side of the desk.

One of the pastors had told him that talking about what happened to Brian could help, that some people found it therapeutic when they'd been through a trauma to talk about it. It gave them a chance to process things, to walk through all the scenarios again in their heads.

"What happened that night?" Marv asked, his face scrunching with concern.

Dave recounted what he knew about the robbery in Albany, about the three young men who had set out to steal some money that night and how they had been armed.

He talked about Brian stopping the white pickup truck, about Kantor gunning him down there in the street. He talked about the three splitting up, and Kantor being unwilling to be taken alive.

He talked about the paramedics and the people at the hospital making heroic efforts to save Brian's life. But Brian was shot through the neck and there was nothing they could do. He was gone before the family even got there to say goodbye.

Marv shook his head. "I'm so sorry, Dave," he said. "Where were you? How did you find out?"

Dave told him about being in Fargo and getting the call and rushing out in the frigid cold and blowing snow and trying to get back to the hospital in St. Cloud as fast as he could without putting himself or other people in danger. And how difficult it was to be separated from his family.

Dave recounted it calmly.

"How are you doing?" Marv asked, slowly, watching Dave's face. "And Lois and the kids, how are they?"

Dave sighed. "Oh, we're doing okay," he said. "We're talking about it. We're leaning on each other. We got some good advice from our pastor. He said everyone's going to grieve differently, so we're trying to respect that and give each other space when we need it. But we're trying to be there for each other too. So it's a balance."

Marv nodded slowly. "How come you're not bitter?" he asked. "How come you're not really upset at those guys who did this?"

Dave was quiet for a moment. "You know, we got some good advice on that, too," he said. "Jason was really angry that first night. Really, really upset. He smashed a picture with his bare hand. But a couple days later he had a talk with one of the monks out at St. John's. Jason said the monk told him we've got two paths we can follow."

Dave put his hands together, then gradually swung one out to the side to illustrate the point. "You can be bitter, you can be unforgiving and you can be really mad at them," Dave said. "But if you go down that road, you're going to be bitter and unhappy, and everyone around you won't like you."

He brought his hands back together and then swung the other one out the side. "Or you can go down that path of forgiveness," he said. "And if you go down that path, you're going to be a positive person, you're going to be able to move on, and you're going to be a much happier individual."

Dave put his hands back on the desk. "So it's better for us if we try to practice forgiveness, no matter how hard it is," Dave said. "Otherwise this could eat us up and destroy our relationships. That's the last thing Brian would want."

Marv nodded.

"That makes a lot of sense," he said. "You know," he went on, "I watched the funeral. And my kids went to the memorial service with us."

"Oh?" Dave said, his eyebrows raised. Marv's kids were fairly young. "What did you tell them about what happened?"

"Well, not to be a follower, first off," Marv said. "You know, I told them about the other two guys . . . what were their names?"

"Ederhoff and Roering," Dave said.

"Right," Marv said. "Ederhoff and Roering. I told my kids about those guys and how they pretty much went along with Tom Kantor and never tried to stop what he was doing. And now their lives are ruined, too."

Dave nodded.

"So I told them, no matter what, if they're with someone doing something they know is wrong, they have to try to stop it," Marv said, pushing an open palm forward for emphasis. "I don't care about peer pressure or anything like that."

"Right," Dave said.

"Then I just told them they have to be willing to forgive and move forward," Marv said. "I told them that things are going to go wrong at some point, and they can't spend their whole lives being angry about it. They've got to be more like you were, up on that altar, telling people not to hate."

Dave smiled. "That's great, Marv," he said. "Thank you."

"Thank *you*, Dave," Marv said.

The conversation stayed with Dave after Marv left his office that day. The pastor had been right: talking about it did help.

Over the next few months that same conversation, with some variations, would play out again and again with different co-workers and clients. The door to Dave's office was always open, and he was surprised at the number of people who would come in and, after a little coaxing, admit they wanted to talk about Brian.

Dave was amazed at the range of people affected by Brian's death. Again, he was thinking about how to harness that for the good of the community.

From early on, it was clear there would be some money available to do that, as well.

Donations poured in to help Wendy and Katelyn build the house Brian had been planning for them. And then still more money came in.

The president of Fingerhut, one of St. Cloud's largest employers, set up a $20,000 endowment for scholarships in Brian's name through the Central Minnesota Community Foundation.

The family set up a scholarship to go to an Alexandria Technical College student each year, because that was where Brian had gone to school. Another annual scholarship was set up for a local high school senior planning to go into law enforcement.

But the Klinefelters wanted to do more. They wanted to do something the whole community could participate in. There were a lot of people affected by Brian's death and a lot who needed to share in the healing as well as the mourning.

Dave also wanted to try to solve a puzzle, a question that kept floating to the front of his mind: how could three young men get to the point where they were willing to participate in an armed robbery and then shoot someone in cold blood?

* * *

BEFORE THAT NIGHT none of the three young men had a background that suggested they were capable of killing a police officer, but there were some warning signs.

Of the three, Ederhoff's brushes with the law were the fewest and least concerning. At age twenty-two, he had been cited for running his car into a homeowner's fence and then driving off. The officer who tracked down the car and made the report the next morning noted that Ederhoff "had a very strong odor of alcohol on his breath," but Ederhoff said he hadn't started drinking until after the collision.

His driver's license was confiscated.

That was in January of 1992. A year later, an officer pulled him over for driving with a broken headlight. After running a few checks, the officer cited him for driving on a revoked license without insurance and giving a false name to police. That earned him a date at the Benton County Courthouse in Foley.

Two years after that, in April 1995, Ederhoff was pulled over and cited again for driving without insurance, this time while leaving his job at a medical supply company in Sauk Rapids. His car was impounded.

That was the extent of Ederhoff's criminal record when, less than a year later, he decided to ride along on an armed robbery with Kantor and Roering.

Roering, though the youngest of the three, had racked up the most extensive police record at that point.

Roering's official address was his parents' house in the small town of Holdingford. But after he turned eighteen, he was spending an increasing amount of time in St. Cloud, cruising the main drag, Division Street, in his white Oldsmobile and hanging out with friends who lived in a neighborhood near downtown.

He was in that neighborhood when he received his first citation as an adult, for playing loud music while he and another young man worked on his car. The tricked-out stereo in Roering's Olds was loud enough to rattle the windows of a house down the street where a thirty-three-year-old man named Donald DeRosier lived.

It was not the first time that had happened, and this time DeRosier lost his temper. He came out of his house with a baseball bat and confronted Roering and the person with him, telling them that if they didn't turn it down, he would smash their speakers.

"Go ahead and do it," one of them said, according to DeRosier. "I'll get a gun and shoot you."

At that point, DeRosier retreated back into his house and called the police.

DeRosier's allegation of the threat could not be verified, but other neighbors vouched for his noise complaint. Roering was written a ticket for violating noise ordinances and given a $100 fine.

Two weeks later, Roering was in trouble again.

While driving around with a car full of people from McKinley Place North near downtown St. Cloud, Roering was stopped by a police officer because he was weaving "carelessly in and out of traffic."

The officer observed four black baton-like items that looked like they could be weapons in the car. Roering told the officer they were windshield squeegees. He said he had found them on the road near a gas station and had removed the heads, leaving just the handles.

"I took the handles for safekeeping," the officer wrote in his report, "as Roering admitted he was using them as weapons for self-defense."

The officer also wrote that he could smell alcohol on Roering's breath and that of several of his passengers. They admitted they had been drinking beer, which one of the passengers said they had snuck out of his mom's refrigerator.

All of them were underage. At eighteen, Roering was the oldest of the crew. The youngest was thirteen.

Roering was cited for underage consumption and written up for a fifty-dollar fine. He missed his court date, just as he had with the one regarding the noise complaint.

A little more than a month later, Roering helped sell marijuana to an undercover police officer.

Again, he was hanging out with a group of people from the McKinley Place North neighborhood. The officer set up the pot deal with one of Roering's friends. Roering drove his friend to the pre-arranged meeting place in a Wendy's parking lot in the white Oldsmobile, which was becoming increasingly familiar to law enforcement.

The officer exchanged fifty dollars for a clear plastic bag that contained a quarter-ounce of what looked like weed. Before he left, he set up a deal for a larger amount in the future. Lab testing confirmed that what the officer received was marijuana.

But the investigation took time, and it was months before a summons was issued for Roering to appear in court, this time on a felony charge.

In the meantime, Roering, still just eighteen, began having regular run-ins with Lance Miller, a sixteen-year-old who, Roering claimed, owed him money.

Miller's mother, Karen, called the police to say that Roering had come to her home, looking for Lance and complaining about bounced checks.

Karen Miller said Roering told her, "I'll get the money from Lance if I have to hold a nine(-millimeter) to his head."

Karen Miller told the police she did not think Roering would follow through on the threat, but she couldn't be sure.

Roering visited the Millers again shortly after his nineteenth birthday.

This time, Lance's father, James Miller, answered the door. Roering told him he was there to talk to Lance about money Lance owed him.

James Miller told Roering he would settle Lance's debt, that he would mail him the money himself. Roering refused to give his address and left.

James Miller called the police.

"Roering has been advised in the past to stay away from their residence due to troubles between him and Lance," the officer who handled the call wrote, adding that James Miller "would like Roering notified not to return to his residence."

The officer called Roering and got his address to give to the Millers so they could settle the debt by mail. He told Roering his only other option was to take Lance Miller to civil court, because if he went to the Millers' house again he would face trespassing charges.

Roering's troubles with the law continued into the summer of 1995. He racked up a couple more minor marijuana– and alcohol-use citations. Then he was involved in a disagreement that escalated into a fight and drew his most serious criminal charges yet.

Roering and some of his friends from McKinley Place were out cruising when another carload of teens started following them. Words were exchanged. The people in the other car would later say it was a case of mistaken identity.

They followed Roering and the others back to the McKinley Place house. Roering maneuvered his car to block them in. The other teens told police that two people, one of whom was later identified as Roering, came out of the car with "crowbars" or "tire irons." They smashed out two windows of the other car and struck a female passenger in the arm before the teens got away and headed to a nearby police station.

Roering would eventually be charged with assault, after police spent months untangling various witness statements and presenting photo lineups.

In October of 1995, Roering had one final run-in with Lance Miller, violating a restraining order.

Karen Miller had signed an affidavit seeking the restraining order against Roering four months earlier. She expressed fear of Roering, who, she wrote, "continues to follow, chase, intimidate, come over to the house after we asked him not to.

"Due to this individual's background and reputation, I ask for a maximum restraining order to keep him away from Lance and our family," she wrote. "He is constantly intimidating in a harassing manner."

Lance Miller told police he was riding his bike to a convenience store near his home that day in October when Roering pulled up alongside him in a car and yelled out the window, "You're dead."

Miller said he took off on his bike and Roering chased him in the car back to his house. Miller and his mother then got in their car and left out the back alley, going to another house to call the police.

St. Cloud police officer Jared Rathbun took the call from the Millers after their October run-in with Roering.

He said that when he called Roering and advised him of the allegations, Roering "immediately became hostile and argumentative."

Roering said he was visiting an aunt who lived near the Millers and had merely gone to the convenience store to make change for a ten-dollar bill. He said he saw Lance Miller there, but did not make contact with him.

According to Rathbun, Roering's father then got on the phone and also "became very hostile and argumentative."

Rathbun told Roering's father that he did not want to speak to him because of his attitude and his son was an adult who could speak for himself.

Roering remained "upset and hostile" after his dad hung up, according to Rathbun, and refused to turn himself in.

Rathbun wrote a ticket for violating the restraining order and put it in the mail. He also called the Stearns County Sheriff's Department and asked them to go out and arrest Roering at his parents' place in Holdingford.

Roering was known to the county sheriff's office.

Two months earlier, it was Roering's parents themselves who had called the sheriff's office to report him for theft. They said he had come home, showered and then left again, with boxes of car stereo equipment in tow.

It was not the stereo equipment they were concerned about, though. Roering's parents told the police that after he left, they noticed that a gun they kept in a drawer was missing—a .44 magnum stainless steel Ruger Redhawk.

"The Roerings had indicated that the handgun was unloaded," the deputy who took the call wrote, "however they did not know if any ammunition, which they do have in the home, was missing. When asked why Kenneth Jr. might want the handgun, they replied they did not know, however he has been arrested for drug possession in the past and they feel that this weapon may be used to obtain cash, either by pawn or other means."

Roering denied taking the gun.

By the end of 1995, all of Roering's legal transgressions were starting to come to a head.

In November, he appeared in court to face charges related to the drug deal with the undercover cop that had occurred more than a year earlier. He took a guilty plea and was sentenced to thirty days in jail, five years supervised probation and a $700 fine.

The district attorney filed assault charges against him January 17, 1996, for the tire iron incident. His arraignment date was set for February 9, 1996.

About a week before his court date on the assault charges, he rolled out with Kantor and Ederhoff to commit the armed robbery that led to Brian Klinefelter's murder.

Kantor's criminal record was slim by comparison.

When Kantor was nineteen, he was convicted of a hit and run after he struck a parked car and took off. The investigating officer said Kantor initially denied his role in the accident, saying he left his keys in the car overnight and woke up to find it damaged.

But the officer was quickly able to draw the real story out of him. "After several minutes of questioning, Mr. Kantor stated he wanted to be honest with me, and admitted that he was driving his vehicle this a.m. and struck a parked vehicle," the officer wrote. "Mr. Kantor states he took off because he was scared. He also states the reason he struck the vehicle was because he couldn't see through his windshield, due to it being frost-covered. Mr. Kantor also informed me that he was on probation and was afraid that any type of arrest would revoke the probation, and he would be sent to jail."

Kantor was on probation because of a burglary he committed in Grand Forks, North Dakota, when he was eighteen.

Kantor had been sentenced to one year at the "State Farm," a prison near Bismark where inmates at one time were sentenced to agricultural work. All but ninety days of Kantor's sentence were suspended, and he got credit for ninety days of time served in the Grand Forks County Correctional Center. So he never had to go to the "farm."

Still, the experience was enough for Kantor to decide he was never going back to jail.

The burglary conviction was also enough to flag Kantor's February 15, 1994, application for a handgun permit, which was denied. That meant Kantor was unable to buy a gun from any federally licensed gun dealer in Minnesota. But that did not stop him from killing a police officer.

* * *

THROUGHOUT 1996, police were investigating where Kantor got the gun he used to shoot Brian Klinefelter to determine if anyone other than Ederhoff and Roering would be charged in connection with the death.

The Klinefelters wanted justice for Brian, but for them justice would come not just in jailing the people involved in his death, but in keeping others from doing the same. They believed that was the legacy Brian wanted—one of peace as well as justice.

The answer to why Kantor, Roering, and Ederhoff went down the dark road they chose the night Brian was killed was not a simple one. Ederhoff and Roering both came from stable homes. Kantor spent time in foster care as a kid, but was adopted out and later restored his relationship with his birth mother.

Dave began to wonder if there was more the community could do to support parents—more that businesses, churches, and law enforcement could do to help them raise their kids.

Dave began assembling a team of people with carefully chosen backgrounds to serve as a board of directors for a memorial foundation that would do charitable work in Brian's name.

Dave would be on the board and so would Wendy. Brad Lindgren would be the law enforcement representative. Pastor Staehling and Sister Coleman O'Connell, a nun wrapping up a ten-year tenure as president of the College of St. Benedict, would provide the religious background.

Jack Amundson, an accountant Dave knew, would represent the business community. So would Greg Reinhart, an executive with First State Bank of St. Joseph, who had started there as an assistant cashier and worked his way to the top.

Marjorie Hawkins was the mother of Jason Klinefelter's fiancée, Angie. She was also a teacher and child development expert who would be the board's educational representative.

Dave was eager to get started. He had realized that getting the foundation up and running was part of his grieving process.

In April of 1996, just three months after Brian died, he assembled the eight board members for their first meeting.

The details were still to be determined, but the mission was clear.

"All right," Dave said. "How do we grow great kids?"

Chapter Sixteen

Dave Klinefelter,
Nineteen Years Later

ALMOST TWENTY YEARS later Dave Klinefelter welcomed a visitor into his home in Sartell.

His was a nice house in a quiet neighborhood, immaculately clean, but not ostentatious. Dave's hair was thinner and mostly white after nineteen years, but he stood straight, walked easily and smiled often.

Lois Klinefelter, Jason Klinefelter, and Jason's now-wife, Angie, waited at a dining table. Behind the table a large window looked out on a small lake—more of a pond, really. The lake was frozen over, and a thick layer of snow covered most of it.

But one area close to the Klinefelter's house had been cleared of snow, leaving a smooth, glassy square of ice surrounded by snow piles.

Dave said one of his neighbors, an ex-hockey player, cleared that section for his kids, who had been skating almost since they could walk.

If Brian were still alive, he might have been the one to clear off the pond for his kids, teaching them how to skate.

But Dave did not mention this. After twenty years, he and the rest of the family had learned to focus on the good times they'd had with Brian, rather than the good times they might have missed out on.

When Dave felt any hint of anger or resentment setting in, he'd think back to Brian's first days in the intensive care unit, the prayers for more time, and the answer that came in the form of almost twenty-six great years.

Dave said he also took solace because Brian was able to live his dream of being a police officer before he died, that he died doing what he loved.

And he was still present.

Dave said that when strangers in Central Minnesota hear his last name, it still causes some to pause and say, "Klinefelter? Are you related to the officer who was killed?"

When Dave says he's Brian Klinefelter's father, the strangers often apologize for bringing up his son's death.

"And I'll say, 'No, actually that's a positive thing, because it means you haven't forgotten Brian,'" Dave said with a hint of pride.

Then he'd get to talk about Brian, which has always been therapeutic for him.

The family's charitable efforts also keep Brian's name circulating.

The foundation still gives two scholarships a year, one to the child of a police officer or other first responder and one to a student training for a job in law enforcement at Alexandria Technical College.

Over almost two decades, the scholarships have peppered Minnesota with police officers who have learned about Brian and how he did the job, and made the case that they could carry on his legacy.

Luke Ahlschlager was one of them.

Ahlschlager, the son of a Vietnam War veteran and a Bronze Star recipient, grew up in a small town in southern Minnesota. After high school, he spent a few years at Southwest Minnesota State University, and then tried to join the military himself.

He was turned away because of a back injury from his high school football days.

Still mulling his next move, Ahlschlager followed a family friend to Alexandria Tech to try the law enforcement program.

His friend ultimately decided to take another path, but Ahlschlager took to police training immediately. He wore a uniform and shined his shoes as if he were in the military, but he was training to comfort people in their time of need, like he had when he worked as a nursing assistant in high school. Police work was the right combination for his instincts for both discipline and compassion.

Ahlschlager never missed a day of school but said he was still surprised when he was named a recipient of the Brian Klinefelter Memorial Scholarship.

As he learned more about Brian, Ahlschlager gained a greater appreciation for what the honor meant.

"You just get a sense he was a very kindhearted kind of guy," Ahlschlager said. "And that's the kind of guy I always wanted to be."

After college Ahlschlager went back home where he got his first police job. It's rarely easy to get started in law enforcement with no experience, and Ahlschlager was convinced having Brian's name on his résumé helped.

"I'm always appreciative of that," Ahlschlager said.

He got his first full-time job in La Crescent, a town of about 5,000 on the Wisconsin border, and he has now served more than a decade there. As one of the seven officers on the force, he has the same sort of relationships with the small-town shop owners that Brian had in St. Joseph.

Ahlschlager married in 2010. He and his wife have four kids and a daycare, which has embedded him even deeper in the community.

"That's kind of my side job, to say the least," Ahlschlager said. "Guys I work with around here say, 'Luke's off, but he's not really off.'"

Ahlschlager said he grew into a man and found his bliss in La Crescent. He and his wife started a family he loved, he had a job he found rewarding, and a community that felt like home.

He says he never forgot what the Klinefelter scholarship did to help make that life, and he was committed to making sure the Klinefelter family was assured it went to the right man and the right police officer.

Years ago Ahlschlager and a friend went to Washington, D.C. They stopped at the Vietnam Veterans Memorial Wall, and Ahlschlager made etchings of the names of his father's fallen comrades.

Ahlschlager also visited the nearby National Law Enforcement Officers Memorial. The names of more than 20,000 officers killed in the line of duty are carved into two curved 300-foot marble walls.

Ahlschlager ran his finger down the marble to the name of Brian Klinefelter. He made an etching of that and mailed it to Brian's family.

* * *

ON THE OTHER SIDE of Minnesota, in the town of Fergus Falls, near Fargo, Matthew Shirkey was one of a handful of investigators on the town's twenty-three-person police force.

Shirkey was in seventh grade when Brian Klinefelter was killed. Growing up with a father who was a cop, he always knew that was a risk of the job, he said. But he didn't really understand the emotional consequences until he heard Brian's story while studying at Alexandria Tech.

"At that point I was a little older, a little more mature and I kind of understood the sacrifice that took place and the effect that has on the family and the kids and the friends and the co-workers," Shirkey said.

He choked up and had to pause to gather himself. He has a wife and two small boys himself.

Shirkey received other scholarships during his time at Alexandria Tech and later at Minnesota State–Mankato, but the Klinefelter award stood out in his mind, in no small part because Dave himself presented it.

There was just something about the fifteen-minute conversation he and Dave shared after the ceremony, Shirkey said. It was so personal, so gentle. Afterward, he felt he was part of the family.

"They're very inviting, very including, and it seems to me from people I've talked to, that's the way Brian was," Shirkey said. "He kind of had this air about him people were drawn to, and yet he wasn't arrogant about it. He was just a very inviting person and truly cared, and that's kind of what I got from Dave."

In 2015, Shirkey had ten years on the force in Fergus Falls, and he had purchased all his equipment from KEEPRS, though he says he's certain the Klinefelters don't feel he owes them anything.

Going to the new store and seeing the mural of Brian smiling and his duty belt on display made Brian's sacrifice—and his family's sacrifice—all the more vivid in Shirkey's mind.

"All I can hope is that if I was to ever be in the eyes of his family or his coworkers, his friends who knew him or who worked with him, that I would hopefully be doing the job up to his standards," Shirkey said. "We think that of a lot of our fallen brothers. It's not to call any of them bad, but it's the good ones that always seem to go the earliest and too soon, if that makes sense."

* * *

DAVE KLINEFELTER'S early vision and drive ensured that the foundation would be more than a scholarship-granting institution.

Over the foundation's first twenty years, some of the board members have changed and so has the official mission statement, but its goal of preventing violence by "growing great kids" remains.

The foundation has handed out thousands of dollars in grants to school anti-drug programs, camps for at-risk kids, faith-based youth programs, and family development initiatives.

But just giving money wasn't enough. Dave and the other board members also wanted to change Central Minnesota's corporate culture to one that recognized the importance of workers staying connected to their children and spending meaningful time with them.

One of the foundation's main focuses became helping businesses create workplaces that are flexible and respectful of their employees' family lives.

The board members developed a list of best practices that Dave called a "tool kit" to help business leaders. Then they honored businesses that put the tools into action.

In 2009, the Brian Klinefelter Family-Friendly Workplace Award went to Netgain Technology, a St. Cloud company that helps small and mid-sized health care providers transition to cloud-based computing.

The company, housed downtown in an imposing, multistory granite building which was built in 1936 and was previously a post office, was founded by Scott Warzecha, now the company's president. In the ground floor lobby, marble floors shared space with polka-dotted carpet, but Warzecha instilled a New Age philosophy within the stone walls.

Netgain's list of corporate values included "Relationships with each other" and "Respect for people."

The company website said Netgain's success was built on teamwork and stated, "We value each person's intrinsic value and uniqueness."

Warzecha started the company in 2000, a few years after the Klinefelter Foundation was up and running. From early on, the company donated to youth-oriented causes.

"I think that comes from just our culture of having a lot of young people, young parents working here," Warzecha said. "They know there's a lot of kids who aren't as fortunate as their kids are, and they like to reach out to them in different ways."

Partnering with the Klinefelter Foundation seemed a natural fit because of its emphasis on kids. Netgain offered the foundation reduced rent on office space and financial contributions in its early years.

Meanwhile, Warzecha was modeling the foundation's corporate initiatives by allowing his employees flexible scheduling so they could go to their children's afternoon dance recitals, coach after-school sports, work around daycare schedules or work from home.

He said he also established a culture in which employees talking on the phone with their spouse or kids—or texting them—during work hours was tolerated or even encouraged.

Warzecha said the accommodations did not hurt his bottom line. In fact, they made good business sense.

"Having that flexibility is how you attract and retain top professionals," Warzecha said. "Good quality employees are also generally good quality parents, brothers and sisters as well. So they're looking for that work/life balance."

Warzecha said the Klinefelter Foundation award was a validation of that approach.

It was one of several awards Warzecha and his company earned for philanthropy and community activism.

Warzecha grew up on the same street as Brian Ederhoff. One of them became a local business leader, the other an accessory to murder. Perhaps nothing illustrated the stakes of the Klinefelter Foundation's mission better than that.

The success of that mission was hard to quantify. Many things went into making a city safe.

But St. Cloud remained one of the safest cities in the Midwest, despite population growth and dramatic demographic changes since the foundation started.

The city became more diverse each year, as a steady influx of Somali refugees joined more longstanding immigrant groups from Latin America and Southeast Asia. The city has had its share of racial tensions, religious divides, and cultural frictions, but there's been remarkably little violence compared to other metro areas of similar size.

The St. Cloud metropolitan area, including parts of Benton, Sherburne, and Stearns counties, had just over 191,000 people in 2013. Its rate of violent crime was about 168 per 100,000 people. Its murder rate was 1 per 100,000.

In Springfield, Illinois, the violent crime rate was 768 per 100,000 and the murder rate was 17 per 100,000. In Saginaw, Michigan, another metro area of about 200,000 people, the rate of violent crime was 752 per 100,000 and the murder rate was 19 per 100,000.

Safe streets and a commitment to community—that was the legacy the foundation intended to carry on in Brian's name.

As St. Joseph grew, as well, newcomers embraced the mission. Joe and Valerie Silva moved to St. Cloud in 2008 and opened a new McDonald's in St. Joseph four years later.

Joe had spent twenty years as a police officer in Chicago, and the family was looking for a charity to get involved in that reflected that background as well as their love for children. Their attorney suggested the Klinefelter Foundation.

After researching the foundation and Brian's story, the Silvas met with Wendy and offered their condolences and their help.

Their restaurant opened in September 2012, but they delayed the grand opening ceremony until the following January to tie it to the seventeenth anniversary of Brian's death and cut a $1,000 check to the foundation.

With Wendy's blessing, they also printed out a series of coupon cards with Brian's picture on them urging customers to "Be Our Best."

Valerie Silva said the idea was to keep Brian's name and example circulating to further the foundation's goal of growing great kids and preventing violence.

The day after the grand opening, she said, one of the workers came up and thanked her and Joe for doing it. His mother was an EMT on site the night Brian was shot, he told her, and she still remembered it like it was yesterday.

"I don't think that name will ever be forgotten in St. Joe," Valerie Silva said.

* * *

SITTING AROUND the kitchen table, Dave and Lois agreed that Dave threw himself into the foundation's work initially as a way to deal with Brian's death. He wanted to take the tragedy and spin it forward publicly almost immediately, using the outpouring of grief as a catalyst for change in the community, to rally people around a cause.

"The tragedy of that evening was Brian being killed, but the tragedy of that evening was also those three young men— one dead and the other two going to prison," Dave said. "How can we, because of this event, do some things that would increase the probability of kids not getting in trouble?"

Dave eventually retired and handed over much of the foundation's duties to his children and Wendy. He remained involved, but the foundation had largely served its personal purpose for him.

It helped him stay positive and reject anger and hate for those who took his son's life.

He said he was not sure how he would feel toward Thomas Kantor if Kantor had survived that night. But he forgave Kenneth Roering and Brian Ederhoff. He was calm—serene almost—talking about them. There was no hint of bitterness, even though he knew both were out of prison.

Dave said he would love to talk to Brian Ederhoff, to try to convince him to use his story about that night to warn kids about the dangers of falling in with a bad crowd and following along with people doing things they know are wrong.

"He would have a great opportunity to tell a story that could affect a lot of young people," Dave said, his eyes lighting up at the possibilities.

Ederhoff showed genuine remorse at his trial, Dave said, while Kenneth Roering showed none.

Still, Dave said, he would also sit down and talk to Roering, if Roering wanted to.

In short, if either wanted to apologize face-to-face for their roles in the events of that night and do what they could to make some good out of it, Dave Klinefelter was ready to listen.

Lois was not so sure. She had supported the foundation's work and believed in what it had done to try to make positive change in the community. But since Brian's death, her focus had always been more inward, on trying to make sure her family was okay first.

Chapter Seventeen

Lois Klinefelter, 1998

Lois Klinefelter walked up the steps of the Stearns County Courthouse, her family by her side.

On April 2, 1998, more than two years after Brian's death, the family was finally going to get some justice. Brian Ederhoff was going to be sentenced for murder as an accomplice, sharing blame for the shots Tom Kantor fired that night.

She looked up briefly at the courthouse's yellow dome before she reached the top step and passed through the high marble pillars that lined the entrance.

The sight had become familiar. They had gone to the earlier proceedings, such as the indictments. They had met with prosecutor Mary Yunker in between her talks with Roering and Ederhoff's attorneys about the possibility of plea deals that would spare everyone a trial rehashing the tragedy. They had gone to the same courthouse five weeks earlier when Ederhoff had told judge Vicki Landwehr he was pleading guilty. Ederhoff, under questioning from his attorney, Paul Engh, had said he would be remorseful for what happened that night for the rest of his life and that, if he could go back and change things, he would do it in a instant.

Roering was still holding out.

As the Klinefelters got settled on the long wooden benches of the courtroom gallery, Lois looked down the line at her family. It had been a difficult couple years for each of them, but she was proud of how they'd stuck together.

There was Greg, who had made several huge changes to his life after Brian's death, including moving back to St. Cloud and becoming a police officer. Jason had gone from a happy-go-lucky boy to a serious, protective man seemingly overnight. And Sarah seemed to have as hard a time as any of them.

Then there was Wendy. The hardest part about their nights together in the aftermath of Brian's death was always at the end, when everyone would hug Wendy, and she would leave. They knew she and Katelyn were going back to an apartment that no longer felt like home without Brian. It was a little better after their house was finished. That was a new place.

But Lois still worried about Wendy. *Thank God for Katelyn*, she thought in those moments. *Thank God for little Katelyn being there with Wendy.*

The gallery was starting to fill up. Some would be news reporters, Lois figured. The family was used to that by now, too.

On the other side of the room another family was filing into one of the benches. Lois recognized the woman as Brian Ederhoff's mother. The woman glanced over briefly, and for a moment their eyes met. Then the other woman looked away and sat down on the bench. She seemed shaky.

Lois looked back at Wendy. She was also shaky, her hands trembling as they tightly gripped sheets of paper. They had decided Wendy was going to give a statement on behalf of the family before Ederhoff was sentenced. Lois hoped it would help her heal.

Lois thought back to more than a year earlier when she and Wendy spent days together planting flowers on the grounds of the hospital where Brian died. Lois ran the floral part of the family landscaping business, and the hospital was one of her biggest clients.

Some asked her that summer if she would be able to do the hospital's flowers that year, just months after Brian died there.

She said she would. It was a job that needed to get done, and she would do it. She would shut out the emotions.

She asked Wendy to join her, and Wendy agreed. The two of them spent the week with their hands in the dirt and the sun on their backs. They had not once talked about Brian's death.

The double doors to the courtroom swung open, and Ederhoff was led in by a bailiff. He still had the same roundish, wire-rim glasses, but he had cut his hair so it no longer fell down to his shoulders. He looked young, pale and skinny.

Judge Landwehr emerged from a door in the back, and the bailiff instructed everyone to rise. Lois turned and watched Wendy again as she gripped the back of the bench in front of her and pulled herself up.

"You may be seated," Landwehr said, and the audience sat as one.

There were a few formalities to take care of first. Judge Landwehr asked both attorneys if they had reviewed the pre-sentence investigation and whether either had any additions or corrections to make before the sentencing.

Both said they'd had adequate time, and neither had any changes to make.

Then it was Wendy's turn to address the court.

She rose, passed by the little swinging gate that separated the gallery from the participants, and stood at a podium, adjusting a microphone in front of her.

The room was silent. The court reporter's fingers were poised above the keyboard, ready to record her words.

"I have put a lot of thought into what I want to say to you today—maybe more importantly, *how* I would say it to you," Wendy began. "How could I possibly put into words the complete devastation the actions of you and your companions have had on that fateful night—what it's caused us? How can I describe to you the incredible husband and father you ripped out of our lives?"

Wendy's voice caught in her throat and she reached up to wipe one of her eyes.

Ederhoff stared down at his hands.

"I wish you could have seen more than a uniform that night," Wendy continued. "I wish you would have seen the big brown eyes that would twinkle when he was up to something mischievous. I wish you would have seen the way that six-foot, four-inch man would so gently cradle his new six-pound baby daughter. I wish you could have heard his infectious laugh. I wish you could have loved and appreciated life like he did because if you would have, maybe you would not be here today. Maybe you would have been able to enjoy the last two years of your life and could look forward to the next twenty-two."

Throughout the gallery came the sound of sniffling and the flashes of white as tissues wiped tears away, but Wendy's voice was getting stronger.

Lois wiped her eyes with a tissue, a deep ache in the pit of her stomach. Wendy had described Brian so beautifully, it was almost like Lois could see him there with her.

"There are no winners in this case," Wendy said. "Your actions have hurt so very many people. But I ask you to think for just a moment of the smallest, most innocent victim in all of this. Our daughter's name is Katelyn. She wasn't even three months old when her dad was killed. She will have not one single memory of her father. She will never know the sound of his voice or be able to feel his big, strong arms around her. She won't even have a letter or a card that her dad wrote especially to her."

Sitting at the defendant's table next to his attorney, Ederhoff looked ashen.

"Some day she will start to ask me questions about him and how he died," Wendy continued. "And I will have to tell her that her dad died over $371 and some liquor. I will have to tell her that on one of the coldest nights in Minnesota's history, her dad lay dying on the middle of the highway."

Lois let her tears flow freely. That had always been the most difficult part for her, imagining Brian lying there in the road, dying.

"I wish I could tell her that you had tried to help him," Wendy said. "I wish I could tell her that you did something, anything, that would have given him at least a chance to survive. Unfortunately, that would not be true. I would like to know that some day I can tell Katelyn you are truly sorry for your actions on January 29, 1996.

"I can't imagine agreeing to spend the next twenty-two years of your life in prison was an easy decision for you. I would like to think that you are taking accountability for your actions on that evening, but at this point I see no evidence of this plea being anything other than a negotiation for a lighter sentence. It would have been gratifying at some point during the past twenty-six months to have had a sincere confession and apology from you. I could have offered this someday to Brian's little girl in the hopes that she could then forgive you for causing her so much pain."

Lois wiped her eyes again and sent up a silent prayer that Wendy would be all right. That Katelyn would be all right. That they all would be.

"Speaking on behalf of Brian's entire family, we hold no ill will toward you," Wendy said. "We are not the only victims of this night. Your parents and siblings must also do without a son and a brother for a very long time. And the next twenty-two years our prayers are that you will become a voice in educating others in helping to prevent this from ever happening again. May God walk with all of us, and I will pray for you. Thank you."

"Thank you, Mrs. Klinefelter," Judge Landwehr said as Wendy walked back to join her family.

Lois felt a sense of pride, through her sorrow. Wendy was barely an adult, but she had shown such grace.

Yunker addressed the court, telling them that though Thomas Kantor was the one who pulled the trigger, Ederhoff and Roering bore responsibility for enabling him that night.

"Mrs. Klinefelter spoke very eloquently about the loss of a husband, a father," Yunker said. "And certainly the Klinefelter family has lost a son, as well as a brother. But there's another victim in this courtroom today, and that is the community of the St. Cloud area."

Yunker said the area had lost a sense of innocence, a peace of mind and a feeling of security.

"And we can't even claim it was some outsider who came in that we are not responsible for," Yunker said. "These young men were members of this community and violated that membership in perhaps some of the most terrible ways. And it is that loss of community, that loss of sanctuary that also occurred on that cold night. For all of these things Mr. Ederhoff is responsible and for all of these things we ask the Court to impose the sentence that has been negotiated here."

Lois squeezed Dave's hand, grateful to have him near. Dave was already working on healing the harm done to the community. He had turned to that so quickly, and the rest of the family, herself included, were following his lead.

Yunker finished and Engh rose to speak.

Engh started by saying that Brian Ederhoff had been remorseful from the beginning, that though he was wearing an orange prison jumpsuit, he was different from other defendants full of machismo and grandiosity who were flippant about their offenses.

"This is a huge mistake in his life," Engh said. "He's fully responsible for it. But he's still a decent young man, and he is, you know, essentially not someone nefarious. He's not someone evil. He made a horrendously bad decision and he's responsible for it."

Lois looked over at Ederhoff's mother, who was in tears. *What would it be like to be her? What would it be like to know your son had done something like this?*

"Just last fall he had a chance in the Little Falls jail to address a class of confirmation kids," Engh said. "And I've never seen this happen before, but thirty fourteen-year-olds came to the jail to hear what he had to say about responsibility and choice in one's life. It's a testament to how he behaved in jail that the kids would be invited to hear him—that a jailer would recommend that they come, and that he would openly discuss the case with these young kids."

Lois could feel Dave gripping her hand more tightly. This was something she knew would affect him—Ederhoff using the story of what happened that night to do some good.

"He talked for two hours, listening to their questions and giving them answers about not only how this happened, but how he was responsible for it and how he was responsible for all his choices and how he got in the car that night and how he made a rational choice to go into that liquor store," Engh said, pacing in front of the judge. "And while we've always pointed out that Mr. Kantor was the shooter, Brian never told these kids he was not responsible for it. He never minimized his behavior. The message he had for the kids, and I think the message he has for everybody from here on out, is that you must pick who you associate with wisely, and he didn't do it that night."

Engh went on, talking about how Ederhoff did not have any prior felonies, that he in fact had no history of violence whatsoever before he went into that liquor store, that he had avoided a rap sheet in his teens and early twenties when other young men who end up spending long stretches in prison usually begin their criminal careers.

"I think the family would like me to convey two things to you," Engh said. "Number one, that Brian is a good boy, which was a quote from his mom. As a mother you always remember the son as a little boy, I guess, but he is a good boy and he's a good young man, too."

He went on to say that the sentence was enormous because Ederhoff would spend the core of his adult life in prison.

There was some fidgeting now on the Klinefelters' bench. Lois looked over and saw Greg shifting his weight and shaking his head a little, scowling. She knew what he was thinking: that Brian, his brother, would never get to experience the core of his adult life at all, in prison or otherwise.

Lois looked again over to the Ederhoff family. Brian Ederhoff's mother was quietly crying.

Engh sat down and Landwehr told Ederhoff to stand. She asked if there was anything he wanted to say before he was sentenced.

"Yes, there is," he said quietly.

"You can proceed," Landwehr said.

Ederhoff took a deep breath. With his eyes still down, he began to speak haltingly. "I would just like to apologize for . . . to everybody, the Klinefelters, for my actions that I was involved in," he said, "And I just . . . I want you to know that . . . that I plan on educating people that make wrong choices. And I apologize to my family for putting their name . . . giving them a bad name, and I am truly sorry. I really am. And I hope God is . . .

God will be with us and get us through these tough times. Thank you."

"Thank you, Mr. Ederhoff," Judge Landwehr said.

She adjusted her glasses and then looked directly at him as she delivered the sentence: twenty-two years in prison.

Ederhoff glanced back at his family as a bailiff snapped handcuffs around his wrists, then gripped his arm and turned him toward the exit. He dropped his head as he was led away.

The Klinefelters hugged each other, the stress of half their judicial battle exiting in one long sigh. Lois looked over to the other side of the room, where Ederhoff's mother was standing and weeping.

Lois extricated herself from her family and walked over. The courtroom hushed, and one of the bailiffs turned to see what was going on. Sensing the possibility of confrontation, he moved toward the two women.

Ederhoff's mother saw Lois approach and looked stricken.

"I'm . . . so . . . sorry," she stammered through her tears.

Lois wrapped her arms around her and pulled her into a long hug. "I'm sorry, too," she said. "Because we both lost sons."

Chapter Eighteen

Lois Klinefelter, Seventeen Years Later

JASON'S WIFE, ANGIE, still clearly remembers Lois sharing that hug with Brian Ederhoff's mother.

Sitting around the kitchen table with Jason, Dave, and Lois, Angie told the story with a note of awe in her voice.

"We were all so young, and, I mean, who does that?" Angie said. "We were struggling. To watch that process, the leadership within a family to step up so we could all move on, that really stuck with us."

The Klinefelter kids and their spouses, themselves now middle-aged and raising children, credit the reactions of Dave and Lois in the wake of Brian's death for ensuring that the tragedy brought the family closer together, rather than tearing it apart.

It was that simple bit of spiritual advice, Lois said, that guided their response. "You can go one of two ways: you can go through bitterness and have it eat you away, or you can go through forgiveness."

From the night Brian died onward, Lois balanced dealing with her own grief with making sure her family members—including Wendy—were okay dealing with theirs.

She had to call Dave to tell him the terrible news, be there with Jason when they found out that Brian didn't make it, and keep an eye on Sarah while she was in denial.

"I found myself being a mom," Lois said.

In the days and weeks that followed, she watched carefully as Jason became more serious, Greg recalibrated his life, and Sarah struggled with the emotions she was suppressing.

Lois was sharing their grief, but at the same time she was frustrated that she didn't really know what they were going through. The dynamic of losing a brother was just different than that of losing a son.

She was closer to understanding the grief Dave was feeling, but it was clear early on that the two of them would deal with their grief differently.

Dave wanted to pivot to creating some public good out of Brian's death, starting almost immediately after the funeral.

Lois needed more time to process things. The whole family could see the difference.

But they remembered their pastor telling them that would happen, and they gave each other the space to grieve in their own ways.

At the same time, Dave and Lois also encouraged the kids to talk about their grief together.

For the first few weeks after Brian's funeral, Lois remembered Wendy and Katelyn would come over almost every evening, and they would all gather in the living room and just talk.

They were in awe at the outpouring of community support and for a while that was what they would talk about, comforting each other with stories about the kindness they had experienced throughout the day.

Then after a couple nights they started to tell stories about Brian, to laugh and have a good time and enjoy each other's company. Lois remembers Sarah struggling with that, but for the rest it felt right. It felt like what Brian would have wanted.

The regular rhythms of life gradually started to return, but with a Brian-sized hole.

Like Dave, Lois was haunted by memories of Brian walking into the kitchen and greeting her. He would throw his huge arm around her shoulder and say, "How are you doing, Mom?"

Dave could talk to people at work about the loss. At first Lois could not. Her landscaping jobs wouldn't start for months.

So Lois poured her energy into making scrapbooks about Brian. She wanted Katelyn, once she got old enough, to know everything possible about her dad and what happened to him.

She collected every news clipping she could get her hands on and pasted them one by one into the scrapbooks, day after day, working for as long as she could stand to read the clippings before grief overwhelmed her and she had to take a break.

Those breaks often included sitting out on the porch with her friend, Kris Boyle, who always seemed to show up just when Lois needed someone to talk to.

One time in the spring, though, it was Wendy who showed up in the middle of the day, lugging Katelyn with her.

"Let's go sit out on the lawn," Wendy said.

It was a beautiful, sunny day, the kind that always lifts the spirits after a long Minnesota winter. The two of them spread a blanket out on the grass and sat there as Katelyn crawled between them.

They talked about the night Brian was killed and cried together. They talked about his life and they laughed a little.

"From that time on it just seemed like we were bonded," Lois said.

The Klinefelters' birthdays are scattered throughout the year, and they had a tradition of getting together almost every month for a birthday dinner. Everyone sat in the same place around the table. They kept that up as the months went on, even though Brian's chair remained conspicuously empty.

Sometimes members of the family would look at the chair and share a glance and questions: should someone sit there? Should the chair be removed?

It was Lois who came up with the answer.

"That place is going to stay empty until Katelyn can sit there in her high chair," she remembered telling everyone firmly.

She also remembered drawing strength from being part of a sisterhood of women whose sons were killed in the line of duty. It was a small, tight-knit group. The number of police officers murdered on the job has steadily decreased since the 1970s, and in Minnesota it was more of a rarity than most states—rare enough that the families recognized each other's names.

Two St. Paul police officers, Ronald Ryan Jr. and Tim Jones, were killed in August 1994, less than two years before Brian Klinefelter's death.

The night of Brian's wake, a woman with dark, curly hair approached Lois and introduced herself as Kelly Ryan, the mother of Ron Ryan Jr.

Lois remembered a long hug and an odd feeling of relief that she was no longer alone.

"It was like, 'Ahhh, somebody amongst all these people understands how I'm feeling,'" Lois said. "Of all these hundreds of people."

They had not met before that night. Their families are close friends now.

The scene replayed itself sixteen years later, but this time it was Lois providing the comfort. She and Dave had arrived at the wake for Tom Decker, a police officer from nearby Cold Spring who was murdered in the line of duty.

They were escorted to a back room where Decker's parents were having coffee. They were introduced and, even after more than a decade, all Decker's mother needed to hear was the last name. No other words were necessary.

"She recognized the name right away, and so she was the same way," Lois recalled. "All of a sudden she knew she wasn't by herself. She said, 'Oh, you know what I'm feeling,' and I said, 'I know exactly what you're feeling.'"

She and Lois have also become friends.

There are still times like that, when the grief is fresh. But Lois found comfort in her family and her faith.

The Klinefelters are still getting together for those monthly birthday parties, but the family keeps growing, and more chairs are being filled.

"I feel that the family became even closer," Lois said. "We used to hug each other once in a while. Now . . ."

She, Dave, Jason, and Angie all laughed.

Dave explained that the family finally had to form hugging lines at the end of the dinners so everyone could be sure they had hugged everyone else before they left. Without the lines it was just too much wonderful, loving chaos.

"As a mom I noticed that my kids never leave, and my grandkids never leave, without hugging and saying 'I love you,'" Lois said.

She smiled.

Like Dave, Lois made an active commitment to practicing forgiveness.

They took that commitment out into the community and shared it in confirmation classes, where teenagers who knew Brian's story sat rapt and absorbed every detail.

"Then there were some adults who came in," Lois recalled. "Everybody wanted to hear the story."

The strength of Dave and Lois's faith, even in the face of tragedy and loss, made an impression on their children.

"I think it was in large part because of Mom and Dad's perspective of it. We never really questioned our faith," Jason said. "We questioned how to make it part of the journey."

Lois said she was not sure she could have been so forgiving toward Thomas Kantor himself, had he lived. It's something she will never know.

But she said that, throughout all the tears over Brian's death, she can't recall ever being angry at God. Just upset that she was not there when Brian died.

"He was alone," Lois said. "That bothered me more than anything."

But he was not alone.

* * *

SIX MONTHS after that conversation around the kitchen table, a white SUV pulled into the Klinefelters' driveway.

A woman with blonde, curly hair stepped out of the driver's seat. It was a sparkling summer day and she wore short sleeves and sandals.

Four children, all of them blond, tumbled out of the vehicle's other doors—three girls and one boy in a tank top.

Dave and Lois Klinefelter waited at the door.

"I had to bring my whole crew," the woman said with a smile, explaining that three of the kids were hers and the other was a friend.

Tiffany Breth was in her mid-thirties, but she did not look much older than that teenage girl who stopped and tried to help Brian Klinefelter on the side of the road.

For years the Klinefelters did not know that part of their son's story. They knew about the nurse who stopped to help, and the first responders. They'd talked to them and to Chief

Lindgren about what they saw that night. But somehow Breth's name had escaped them.

She had testified at some of the court proceedings for Ederhoff and Roering, but Lois and Dave did not remember her. Those had been long, stressful days.

So the Klinefelters were meeting her for the first time, almost twenty years after she tried to help their son.

The kids got comfortable in the family room watching TV, while Dave, Lois, and Tiffany went into the adjoining room and sat down at the kitchen table.

Tiffany told them about driving through St. Joseph that night, how much different it was now, how much had changed. There were no houses in 1996. No McDonald's. It was a largely deserted stretch of road.

Small talk. It was a little awkward making the transition to talking about what they were all thinking about. But Lois needed to hear it.

"Did you see what happened?" she asked.

"Yes and no," Tiffany said.

She paused. "I don't know how much you want me to tell," Tiffany said.

"Were you actually the first person there?" Lois said.

Tiffany nodded and then, in a lilting Minnesota accent, the story began to pour out of her.

She talked about driving back from work in the bitter cold and seeing the white pickup pulled over on the other side of the median, with the police officer at the driver's door.

She talked about seeing the police officer suddenly fall and the truck peel away, and told the Klinefelters she did not know Brian had been shot.

"I just thought, ya know, maybe something happened to him and they thought, 'Here's my free getaway,'" she said.

She talked about making the U-turn and heading back toward the fallen officer, parking her car so it would shield his body. She talked about going to him and trying to comfort him, but he was bleeding and nonresponsive.

She talked about the other police officer arriving and her telling him over and over again about the white truck that just drove away.

"Of all the reports, I thought it was just the one person, the nurse," Lois said. "I never knew about you."

Lois raised her glasses and wiped her eye with one finger.

"The biggest thing I thought that night is I didn't want him to die alone," Lois said. "It was so cold. I just think God sent you."

Her voice caught as she started to choke up. She recovered long enough to say, "I just have to thank you."

Tiffany nodded sympathetically, her blue-green eyes filling with tears as well.

"Oh, no, he wasn't alone," she said gently.

She said that when she learned the Klinefelters wanted to meet her, to talk to her, because Lois Klinefelter had been thinking all these years that her son was alone that night, she started thinking about her own children and cried.

"I can't even imagine," she said.

Lois asked her how a seventeen-year-old girl had the courage to react the way she did that night.

"I don't know," Tiffany said, shaking her head. "But there was not even a moment of hesitation. I didn't even think about it. I didn't want somebody else racing down the road to hit him."

"Every winter, when it gets cold, that's what I think of," Lois said. "How cold it was that night."

The three of them moved on to talk about the aftermath, the police questioning Tiffany, the court dates. She said she testified twice.

Dave had been silent through most of the conversation, though he did get up once to grab a box of tissues. His eyes were damp as well.

"We should have talked to you at the court," he said, wondering how their paths had failed to cross.

"I don't remember much of the trial at all," Lois added. "It was just a blur."

There was a pause in the conversation.

Dave pushed himself up from the table and fetched a picture of Katelyn.

"This is Brian's daughter," Lois said. "She's in her second year of college now."

Tiffany's eyes widened. "Ohhhh," she said in disbelief as she lightly touched the photo. "How old . . . ?"

"She was two months old," Lois said.

"That's all?" Tiffany said. "She's very pretty."

Dave and Lois told Tiffany about all-family vacations and the birthday dinners and about how tightly bonded the family had become since Brian's death.

Then they asked what had happened in her life since that night. Tiffany still lived in Central Minnesota, but out in the country, farther from St. Cloud.

After high school, she went to college for a bit, then worked at a law firm. She met her husband, also from Minnesota, in Mazatlán while they were both vacationing. He delivered cars to dealerships and she stayed home with the kids.

She said she was not traumatized by seeing Brian killed. It all happened so quickly, she wasn't sure she really had time to take in and process what she had truly witnessed.

But she had never forgotten it, either. "Throughout the years you kind of think about it," she said. "Drive through that part of St. Joe and it kinda pops into your mind."

She said she was also a Christian and agreed with Lois that she was meant to be on that road that night. "I'm a firm believer God puts people in our paths for a reason," Tiffany said.

The visit lasted more than an hour, and finally it was time for Tiffany and the kids to head home.

Lois had made cookies, though, and Dave got them from the freezer and softened them in the microwave. As he passed them out to the kids, Lois and Tiffany shared a long hug in the entryway between the kitchen and the living room.

"Thank you," Lois said.

"I'm glad I could ease your mind a little," Tiffany said.

* * *

WHILE TIFFANY BRETH was visiting the Klinefelters, she also asked about Wendy. It was the question that most vexed those who remembered Brian Klinefelter's story: what became of the police officer's beautiful young widow, the one left to raise their infant daughter on her own?

The Klinefelters understood because they themselves spent many nights worrying about what would become of Wendy.

Lois remembered a fateful conversation she had with Brian after he watched the funerals of Ron Ryan Jr. and Tim Jones on television. He came over and started talking about all the people in the crowd and wondering what it would be like if he were the officer in the casket.

"Oh, Brian, don't talk like that," Lois remembered saying. "Nothing's going to happen."

But then Brian got very serious and made his mother look him straight in the eye.

"Mom, will you and Dad promise that, if anything happened to me, you'd take care of Wendy?" Brian said.

Tears came to Lois's eyes. "Brian, nothing's going to happen," she repeated.

"No," Brian insisted. "Promise."

"Okay," she said. "We promise we'll do that."

Lois remembered that conversation in the weeks following Brian's death, when she watched Wendy leave their driveway and head back to her apartment that would seem so empty without Brian's smile, without his laugh.

"We prayed constantly she would find somebody in her life who would understand the role she had to play the rest of her life with law enforcement," Lois said. "God answered that prayer."

Chapter Nineteen

Wendy and Katelyn, 1999

IN THE SUMMER of 1999, Wendy Klinefelter was trying to decide if she was ready to date again.

Jason wanted to set her up with a friend of his, another cop. His name was John, and he was starting a K-9 program in the St. Cloud Police Department. Jason rode with him occasionally, and they'd really hit it off. He and Angie wanted to invite Wendy and John over for dinner—a couples' date night.

"Are you interested?" Jason asked.

Wendy was not sure.

The fact that John was a cop was not a problem for her. She'd studied criminal justice. She'd felt firsthand the love and camaraderie the law enforcement family poured out to her after Brian died. Police work got in your blood, and it was in hers.

For her the question was more whether she was ready for a relationship with someone else. It had been three years since Brian's death. In some ways it felt like it hadn't been that long, and in other ways it felt like a lifetime.

She was definitely ready to move forward with some aspects of her life. The legal process, for example. She wanted that to be over.

Brian Ederhoff's plea and sentencing had taken two years, but that had been swift justice compared to the legal process with Kenneth Roering Jr., who had fought the murder charge every step of the way. Roering had finally gone to trial in September 1998, after the proceedings were moved to Duluth. The prosecutors had asked Wendy and the Klinefelters to be in the courtroom, to support the prosecution and provide the jurors with a living reminder of the crimes committed that night. They were there, nearly every day, listening to the witnesses reliving it.

When the jury returned a unanimous guilty verdict, it seemed like it was over.

Then something happened that shocked everyone. One of the jurors slipped the bailiff a note to give to the judge. It had two words on it: "I lied."

The note caused an uproar in the court. No one knew how to proceed. The judge scheduled a new hearing to determine whether the verdict would stand.

The juror went to the media and said she'd never wanted to convict Roering of murder because he wasn't actually the triggerman. She said she felt pressured into it by the other jurors.

Months later, when the parties reconvened, the judge declared a mistrial. The prosecutors appealed, but the state Supreme Court declined to review the ruling. The guilty verdict was gone.

Legal scholars would debate the odd outcome for months. But for Wendy and the Klinefelters, it was not academic. It was their lives, and it meant gearing up for a whole new trial.

The prosecutors brought charges again in June 1999, but by then Wendy was ready to be done.

The prosecution came to her and the Klinefelters and said they had a possible plea deal with Roering's defense. He would get about nineteen years, and he would have to serve at least thirteen of it, even with good behavior. But he would get credit for time served, which at that point was more than three years. So he could be out in ten years.

Ederhoff's sentence would be reduced to match that, the prosecutors said. It would look bad if the guy who pleaded guilty first got more time. This would be the fairest way.

Did it seem like justice for Brian? Not really. But Wendy and the others didn't object. They just wanted to move on.

Wendy was determined not be bitter or angry. She made a conscious decision not to let Brian's murder do that to her.

Those first few weeks she was just numb, in shock, not believing it. Then, after months of not seeing Brian, not talking to him, his death became real and the ache in her heart was almost unbearable.

Brian was the only man she'd ever loved, and in the seven years from when they started dating until the day he died, they had barely been apart.

She had been a freshman in high school when they met; he was a junior. He had a crush on one of her friends, but that friend already had a boyfriend. So she introduced Brian to Wendy.

He was tall, she remembered, and had kind eyes. And that smile. Everyone noticed that smile.

He had announced his attraction to her in typical high school boy fashion, by tripping her in the hallway. When they would tell the story years later, Brian would embellish it by saying, "Then she put me in a headlock." It usually got a laugh.

Wendy's mom thought she was too young to go on "car dates" at the time, so Brian would come to the house. From then on, they were all but inseparable. Wendy was a serious person, and he made her laugh. He was responsible, but still a kid at heart.

Wendy sighed at the memories. Three years later it still hurt. There was still a void. She wondered if there always would be.

She looked down at Katelyn, now almost four years old, playing on the floor. She saw more and more of Brian in her every day, and there was some comfort in that.

They hadn't intended to have a baby when she got pregnant with Katelyn. They'd only been married about a year. Wendy was still finishing school and Brian was still getting settled at work. They wanted to buy a house before they started a family.

She cried when she told Brian she was pregnant. But he had grinned, all excited, and told her not to worry. "This is a good thing," she remembered him saying. "It's okay."

From that point on, it was all good.

Thank God for Katelyn, Wendy thought.

After the numbness wore off and she started to accept that Brian was really gone and not coming back, it was Katelyn who kept her going. Katelyn was her reason for getting up in the morning for a long time.

She was a distraction from the pain, and she was a pure, beautiful, living piece of Brian.

When the bitterness started to creep in, and the anger started to tear at her, there was a mantra Wendy would repeat: *Positive, Brian, Katelyn.*

She could not let herself become angry or bitter, because she had to raise Katelyn, and she had to raise her in a way that would make Brian proud.

Still, it wasn't easy. She wondered sometimes how she would have coped if Thomas Kantor had survived that night. She didn't know how she would feel if he were still alive, even in prison.

The other two—she thought they'd made terrible decisions that night and were cowardly for not trying to stop Kantor from shooting Brian or at least getting out of the truck and trying to help him afterward. But they were followers.

No, she would not waste too much energy being angry with them. But sometimes it was hard not to be angry with God.

Wendy's family was very Catholic. One of her grandmothers even expressed some concern about her marrying a Lutheran, until she met Brian and quickly came to love him. Brian had that effect on people.

But lately Wendy was finding little comfort in her Catholicism.

Brian so wanted to be a dad. He was so excited about it. He was so good at it. Why God would take that away from him after just a few months, she could not fathom. It wasn't fair.

They had almost bought a house in Avon before Brian died. It was out in the middle of nowhere, with lots of land and a driveway that stretched for almost a mile. They loved it, but someone else bought it out from under them, paying cash.

Now, of course, she was glad the sale hadn't gone through. The thought of being way out there with a baby and without Brian made her shudder.

Missing out on that house was a blessing in disguise, but then, God kind of owed her one.

Three years before Brian was killed, Wendy's sister Jackie died of brain cancer. Jackie was only eleven. Then Wendy's childhood home burned down, and the family lost most of its momentos of Jackie in the fire.

Then Brian.

Then, two years after Brian's death, while the trials were still going on, Wendy's mother died of cancer.

At that point it felt like God was picking on her. It was egotistical to think like that, she knew, but she couldn't help it sometimes. She saw other people who seemed to skate through life with relatively little tragedy and some, like her family, that had to weather death and disaster, only to have it happen again.

It made her wonder how an all-powerful God could make those decisions, how he decided where to sprinkle that around, dumping on some and leaving others unscathed. She had tried to live a good life.

Wendy needed to talk about Brian, even three years later, which was tough for some people to understand. At first everyone knew she was still mourning. But after the first year or so she discovered there was a growing expectation that she "get over it."

But the memories were still so fresh and the ache came with the memories. Acknowledging the hurt, talking about it, made it a little more bearable.

She could still talk to her siblings, and she could still talk to the Klinefelters. They all understood the pain. They were all still willing to talk about Brian.

She was so thankful to them for embracing her the way they had, for enfolding her into their circle of unconditional love.

Lois had sat with her out on the lawn and talked and cried while Katelyn played in the grass.

Dave had gotten her involved in the foundation. She had followed his lead on that, understanding his need to use Brian's life to create some sort of positive change in the community.

She was more focused on raising her child and finishing school. But the foundation gave her opportunities to talk about Brian.

And she'd become closer with Brian's brothers, too.

Greg and Jason were getting ready to go into business together with her, at KEEPRS.

She had retail experience and a criminal justice degree. Jason had studied business, and Greg knew marketing. Between the three of them, they had the makings of a well-rounded, if young, management team.

At KEEPRS, she would be able to work every day with her Klinefelter family and stay in contact with her law enforcement family as well.

So they were going to do it. They had the business plan, they had the storefront, they were working on inventory. The place needed some work, but she didn't mind that.

The trials were finally over, and KEEPRS seemed like a good answer to the question: "What are we going to do now?"

Life would never be the same without Brian, but the sun would keep coming up and she had to make the most of the days she was given.

Wendy scooped up a now-slumbering Katelyn off the floor and carried her to bed, tucking her in and kissing her gently on the forehead.

She crept out slowly, closing the door noiselessly behind her. Then she walked back to the living room and picked up the phone to call Jason. She'd decided she wanted to meet his friend John.

Chapter Twenty

Wendy, John, and Katelyn, Sixteen Years Later

O N A PERFECT summer day in Minnesota, Wendy sat on the front porch of Dave and Lois's home in Sartell. The shrill sounds of children arguing wafted over from across the street, briefly disturbing the peaceful neighborhood.

"Those kids sound like mine," Wendy said.

Then she laughed.

Wendy Klinefelter was now Wendy Klinefelter Tragiai. That first dinner with St. Cloud Police officer John Tragiai turned into many more dinners and, about a year later, a wedding.

That day on the porch, sixteen years later, Wendy and John had just gotten back to Sartell after dropping Katelyn off at college in Mankato. Their two other children, Jack and Elise, waited at home.

Wendy was the picture of summer in capri pants, a flowery blouse and flip-flops, with a pair of sunglasses perched on her head. She was in her forties but looked much the same as she did twenty years earlier, except that her hair was straight rather than wavy.

Her smile still gleamed, but there was a subtle difference there, too. In the pictures of her and Brian holding Katelyn there was a giddiness to her smile, something carefree about it.

That was replaced by a more tempered, but just as genuine, smile, the smile of someone who knew loss was part of life but for now felt safe and contented.

Wendy said she found her place in the world as a mother.

She was still involved in the foundation and in KEEPRS, but she allowed both to take a backseat to raising her children now.

Jason was the president of the foundation's board of directors at that time, Wendy the vice president. And John was president of KEEPRS, though she remained a majority owner.

John was there from the company's beginnings. Wendy remembered him helping them build fitting rooms for officers to try on uniforms before the store even opened, when the two of them had just started dating.

Once it opened, KEEPRS took off faster than any of them had expected. The plan hatched in the Duluth hotel room, with Wendy running the business, became more of a time commitment than she was willing to make.

"I knew I couldn't be the mom I wanted to be and run the whole thing," she said.

They needed a general manager, and John was starting to experience burn-out after almost eight years as a cop. He took a six-month sabbatical to take over KEEPRS' day-to-day operations and never went back.

Wendy said she remained proud of the work KEEPRS did and the way its employees and customers were treated. She was glad to maintain a personal connection to law enforcement.

But stepping back from the day-to-day operations to focus her energy on motherhood still felt like the right choice.

"I figured out that, of all my jobs, that continued to be my most important," Wendy said. "I'm responsible for these three people becoming productive members of society who follow in Brian's footsteps rather than the other side of that story. To me that's been number one."

That didn't mean Wendy blamed the parents of Thomas Kantor, Brian Ederhoff, and Kenneth Roering Jr. for Brian's death.

In fact, her father knew Thomas Kantor's adoptive parents before Brian was killed. She said they were good people who did their best.

"They, I think still to this day, feel terrible," Wendy said. "It's not their fault obviously."

As for Roering and Ederhoff, Wendy didn't spend much time thinking about them or what they might be doing now, though she knew they were out on parole. She hoped, for the sake of the community, that prison had changed them for the better, not the worse.

But she didn't waste anger on them.

They were followers, along for the ride, with poor taste in friends and too weak to stand up for themselves or Brian.

"So pointless," she said, shaking her head. "Such a waste. So many lives."

Wendy rebuilt her life, to the extent she could.

She still missed Brian. She always would. But John is okay with that.

"I marvel at his ability to handle it," Wendy said. "He stepped into a very difficult situation. Not only all the pain and all the baggage I brought with, but also that I'm very connected to Brian's family, so he had to be willing to accept that."

John was at Wendy's side in a 2013 picture of her and Dave and Lois accepting an oversized check from the Silvas's McDonalds on behalf of the foundation. Solidly built, with a stubbly beard and short, spiky hair going gray around his ears, John had a smile so broad it made his eyes squint.

Wendy said he makes her laugh. He was like Brian in that way, but he was not trying to be Brian.

It was a tough needle to thread emotionally—trying to make Wendy happy while understanding that part of her life would always be remembering something very sad.

"He does it remarkably well," Wendy said. "He is very respectful of my past and where I've been and what I've gone through and trying to make the best of my future. He feels so bad for Katelyn and me and what we lost. He will say he never will replace Brian, but he is trying to make it as wonderful a life as possible for us and he's done an amazing job. Not many people could handle what he's handled."

* * *

JOHN TRAGIAI'S first solo shift as a St. Cloud Police officer was the night Brian Klinefelter was killed.

Tragiai grew up in one of the Twin Cities suburbs. After graduating high school in 1990, he went to St. Cloud State University to study broadcasting. He had already been in some high-level theater productions and done some commercials. His mom thought he would make a great newscaster, like Dan Rather.

John joined the police reserves while he was in St. Cloud, though, and quickly took to law enforcement instead. He added a criminal justice minor and started working for the Stearns County Sheriff's Department's water patrol program.

For one year there he worked alongside Brian Klinefelter, before Brian got a job with the St. Joseph Police Department.

Shortly after Brian left for St. Joe, John got a job with the St. Cloud Police Department. He went through all of the field training, riding with other officers. Then, on January 29, 1996, he got to go out on his own for the first time.

John said he has a bad memory in general, but the details of that shift remain vivid almost twenty years later.

He was sitting in the office writing some reports when he heard the dispatcher say, "Thirty-one, thirty-two, thirty-three copy, agency assist."

"I remember immediately thinking, 'Oh, my gosh, this has to be something serious," John recalled. "I've never heard dispatch call for three officers for an agency assist.'"

It was serious. A St. Joseph officer had been shot, and the suspects were still on the loose.

John said he remembered speeding down Division Street with his lights flashing and sirens blaring, yelling in frustration when cars in front of him were slow to get out of the way.

The night was chaotic. More information kept coming through the radio, and he and other officers were trying to navigate areas in northwest St. Cloud that were newly annexed and largely unfamiliar. Eventually he ended up on Benton Drive in Sauk Rapids, responding to the scene where Nancy Wiggin had shot Tom Kantor.

When he got there, he spotted a Sauk Rapids officer he knew, standing like a statue with his foot over a gun, holding a shotgun.

"I ran up to him and said, 'Tell me it's not Brian that was shot,'" John remembered. "And he said 'It is.'"

When John left the scene, there was still some hope Brian might survive the shooting.

But as he was driving back into St. Cloud, a message came onto his computer screen: "St. Joe Police Officer Brian Klinefelter is 10-72."

Ten-seventy-two. Dead.

John pulled his squad car into the nearest gas station and put it in park. He wept.

* * *

ABOUT THREE YEARS later, John was riding with Jason Klinefelter in his squad car when Jason asked John if he'd like to be set up on a blind date.

"I said 'sure,'" John remembered. "'With who?' And he said Wendy."

John was surprised, but quickly said yes.

John said he had felt an unusual sense of responsibility to do something for Wendy ever since Brian died. He revealed something he had not told anyone, even Wendy: he thought Wendy was Lutheran, so in the months following Brian's death he went to Lutheran services around the area, hoping to run into Wendy at church.

He said he just wanted to tell her he and the law enforcement community were there to support her if she needed anything.

"Of course I never ended up seeing her at any church service," John said.

Then, years later, Brian's brother decided to set them up.

They had dinner at Jason's house, and he took Wendy to the Dairy Queen before dropping her off at her house. He said it was innocent, platonic even, but they enjoyed each other's company and wanted to see more of each other.

He still remembered the first time he came over to Wendy's house, rang the doorbell and saw little three-year-old Katelyn, all dressed up, there at the door with her mom.

"She was just so beautiful," John said. "I knelt down and said, 'Oh, do you wanna see my dog? My police dog?' And she wasn't quite sure, but then she did. You know, it was a neat start of a relationship."

John started coming over to Wendy's for dinner in the middle of his shift three or four times a week. She would wait up for him, keeping everything warm, so they could share it together at 9:00 p.m. Sometimes he would get a call five minutes before he was supposed to go to her place, and he'd have to tell her he might not show up for a while.

She always understood.

"Sometimes at eleven o'clock at night I'd pull up in my squad and take my dinner break and still she would have waited and we'd have dinner at eleven o'clock at night," John said. "That just goes to show you what kind of woman she is."

He paused.

"She's the strongest woman I know. I don't know what I ever did to deserve her."

John said he never saw himself getting married and certainly never saw himself being a father. But he fell in love with Wendy and Katelyn, and from the moment they became a family, he made a commitment to be the best husband and the best father he could, for Brian's sake as well as theirs.

It was not always easy, living in Brian's shadow. He could admit that.

When he and Wendy were still dating, another officer found out and tried to put a stop to it.

"Don't you dare," John remembered the officer telling him. "She's sacred ground."

John said Wendy was furious when she found out.

Throughout their marriage, John measured himself against Brian's standard. And it was impossible to know if he was meeting it.

"Sometimes you feel like you've done a good job and Brian would be proud," John said. "Sometimes you wonder if Brian would have been here, would he have done a better job."

Katelyn grew up asking often to hear stories about "Daddy Brian" and John would oblige, because he wanted those memories always to be a part of her life.

Gatherings at the Klinefelter house would also often turn to talk of Brian, and John would get a little quieter than usual. He was human, and the bitterness of being in Brian's shadow sometimes crept in, no matter how hard he tried to suppress it.

"It's something I've tried really hard to hide, both from Wendy and Katelyn," John said. "And the Klinefelter family, too, to be honest. I try to keep those emotions inside. Those emotions . . . in my opinion those emotions are very selfish, so I would rather share the emotions of support and love."

A sort of survivor's guilt, sometimes, goes back all the way to when Brian was first killed, and John read about his widow and his little girl in the newspapers.

Why couldn't it have been me? John remembered thinking. *I don't have a family, I don't have a kid, I don't have a wife. Why couldn't he have taken me instead of him?*

To this day, John has no answer to that. No one does.

It was just the way things happened.

It helped that the Klinefelter family accepted him and that Dave and Lois have told him many times how much they appreciate his presence in their lives, and in Wendy and Katelyn's lives.

They treated him like one of their sons.

Katelyn's enduring love also helped ease his mind. One of John's great fears as he was raising her was that, someday, when she was older, she would turn to him and say, "You can't tell me what to do. You're not my real dad."

That would have been crushing.

"She's never said that," John said. "We've had a very open relationship, and there's always been 'Daddy Brian' and me, her dad here on earth."

John knows Katelyn and her mom will always have a special bond that he doesn't share, but the three of them, and Jack and Elise, have formed a happy family anyway in part by making each other their top priority.

John said it was a common misconception that he gave up police work because Wendy asked him to. The truth, he said, was that it was entirely his idea and ultimately his decision.

He was feeling pulled in a million different directions as St. Cloud's first K-9 officer, and he wanted to re-prioritize his life so he could put his family above all.

To this day he often misses being a beat cop, but as president of KEEPRS, he was able to serve the law enforcement community in a broader way.

He believed he made the right decision, both for himself and for Wendy, Katelyn, Jack, and Elise.

He said he fell short as a husband and a father sometimes. But he tried really hard, even when it meant putting his own emotions aside.

"I just . . . I wanted the best for Wendy and Katelyn," John said. "So I tried to make it all about them, as much as I could."

* * *

SETTING UP his brother's wife with another man was not a decision Jason Klinefelter took lightly.

"Did I think about it? Certainly," Jason said. "Did I question whether or not it was the right thing to do? I know I asked myself that. But the thing about it was, Brian was gone. What you saw and what you were left to deal with on a daily basis was the hole."

Everyone who knew Jason said he did years' worth of growing up in the days following Brian's death.

He said part of that maturation was making a commitment to protect Wendy any way he could.

He tried to be there for her. But he could see she was lonely, especially on the weekend nights when she was holed up at home, just her and Katelyn.

There was a role there that he could not fill.

Jason knew Brian as well as anybody, and he knew that Brian would not want to see Wendy that way. Brian loved and adored Wendy, and he would want her to find another companion.

"At that point in time that kind of trumps, you know, any personal feelings about somebody replacing your brother," Jason said.

So Jason set up the dinner, and any reservations he might have had about the decision soon vanished.

In John he saw someone who had a compassionate heart, someone willing to look past the tragedy in Wendy's life and see her for who she was, rather than only as Brian Klinefelter's widow.

Like Jason's brother, John was gregarious and fun to be around. He could bring joy back into Wendy's life, and Wendy was ready for that.

"I remember how excited she'd get just to have dinner with him," Jason said. "Just to make him a dinner when he was on duty and have somebody to wait for, I guess."

John's growing presence did not diminish Brian's role in Wendy's life, or her role in the Klinefelters' lives. John came to all the family functions and he was there as they shared stories about Brian and sometimes shed tears.

Jason said it's been that way since the beginning.

"The remarkable thing about John all these years is he's never once asked not to be part of that or not allowed the memory of Brian to exist," Jason said. "He's been completely willing to accept that as very much a part of all of our lives."

As John accepted the Klinefelters as part of his family, the Klinefelters accepted him as part of theirs. Lois and Dave consider him a son-in-law and Jack and Elise are as much their grandchildren as Katelyn.

Three families melded into one, Wendy said, and she loved that her children all have aunts and uncles and cousins who genuinely care about them and are involved in their lives whether they're related by blood or not.

Katelyn was been one of the beneficiaries of all that love.

After they dropped her off at college in Mankato, Wendy and John talked on the way back about how hard they tried to give her the best life they could.

"We weren't perfect parents," Wendy said she told him. "But we have a really good kid, so we must have done something right."

* * *

KATELYN TRAGIAI went skydiving on Father's Day 2015.

"I asked my dad John to come with, and he was like 'There's no way. There's no way I'll jump out of a plane,'" Katelyn said, grinning. "But then when I was talking to my grandma Lois, she goes, 'That's crazy. That's something your dad would totally want to do.'"

Katelyn wore a special t-shirt that day. It was one from Brian's memorial service with his badge on it that her godfather had saved for her. She had kept it preserved her whole life, never wearing it for fear of ripping or staining it. But that day, when she was going to be up in the clouds, felt like the right time to finally put it on.

Katelyn said she had two dads, one in heaven and one on earth. She does not call John her stepdad or her adoptive dad. He's just Dad.

But Brian is "Dad" also. She says usually people know which dad she's talking about based on context, but sometimes she has to say "my dad John" or "my dad Brian" for clarity. And sometimes when she's talking amongst family, she still says "Daddy Brian."

"It sounds silly now that I'm nineteen years old, but that's just what I've always said," Katelyn said.

Katelyn grew into a beautiful mix of her mom and dad, with Wendy's high cheekbones and Brian's jaw and big smile. There's one more facial feature she inherited from her father: his thick eyebrows.

"But I pluck them," Katelyn said with a laugh.

Katelyn couldn't remember exactly when she was told what happened to her father. She grew up knowing the outlines of the story, and knowing that her grandparents on the Klinefelter side were not her dad John's parents, but her dad Brian's parents.

She grew up knowing Brian was someone special, someone who touched a lot of people in a short time.

She saw the park named after him and heard the stories from people who her father had helped in some way. It was a source of pride, and also a source of pressure.

"Going through my teenage years, I felt like I could never mess up like other teenagers," Katelyn said. "I felt I couldn't go out and drink or do all that kind of stuff, 'cause I didn't want to ruin his name and his legacy or anything like that."

Katelyn embraced the legacy as something much more important than sneaking a beer underage.

A couple of years ago she created a Facebook page for people to share their memories of Brian so she could get to know him better.

More than 800 people joined, loading it up with pictures and stories.

"That was great," Katelyn said with a smile. "I read them all."

The posts have died down now, but there's still a rush of them every year on Brian's birthday, the anniversary of his death, and during law enforcement memorial week. Often people share what they were doing when they found out Brian had been shot.

Wendy said Katelyn was blessed with two dads watching over her, and Katelyn said she felt the same way. She loves John and can barely remember a time when he was not in their lives.

But those early years did imprint on her, on some level, a feeling of admiration and loyalty to the mother who kept everything together for her sake during those dark days.

"We've always had a closer bond," Katelyn said. "I'm close with my dad, but most of my friends are daddy's girls and I'm a momma's girl. Because we spent the first three years of my life together, alone."

In the summer of 2014, Katelyn was in Europe for a class, and John surprised Wendy by buying her a plane ticket to go visit.

Mother and daughter visited Rome, Florence, Barcelona, and Paris together. By that time, Katelyn had already been to Paris once but wanted to go back and share it with Wendy. It was one of her favorites places.

They watched the Eiffel Tower light up as day turned to night and ate crêpes from a nearby stand. "It was so good," Katelyn said. "Nutella and banana and strawberries."

Katelyn believed Brian was there, too, that he's always with her.

Sometimes at night she prayed to God and to her dad at the same time. It was something she did since she was quite young, though she admitted that, through the years, she'd had times when she questioned her faith.

She was raised Catholic, but for most of her childhood the family only rarely went to church, and when they did she did not feel like she got much out of it.

As she got older, she started to ask herself why she believed what she did, and some of the answers scared her.

"I only felt like I believed in God because I knew that my dad was in heaven," Katelyn said. "I had to know that my dad was in heaven and in order to talk to my dad I had to believe in God at the same time."

Then she was asked to work in the nursery at the church her aunt Sarah attended.

When she walked into the Waters, the atmosphere was totally different than what she was used to. The music was more contemporary. The pastor made the Bible relevant to her daily life, and the place just seemed warm and inviting.

Wow, I have to come back here, she remembered thinking.

Katelyn was in the middle of confirmation classes in her Catholic church. But as soon as she was confirmed, she started going to the Waters instead.

"I got to know God better, and now we're all good," Katelyn said.

It was not an easy transition for her family. She went alone at first, then finally convinced John to come.

He cried the first time he went, she said.

So then John starting going, too, and bringing Elise and Jack. Wendy's resistance lasted a little longer, but Katelyn understood.

"She's had her roots in the Catholic church for a long time," Katelyn said. "She finally switched over and now we're all happy."

* * *

WENDY ACKNOWLEDGED that Katelyn changed the family's spiritual life dramatically by connecting them to the Waters.

"I have to thank her for getting us there," Wendy said. "We had just stopped going to church."

She also credited John for taking the lead spiritually, something she felt like she could no longer do.

Wendy said she never stopped believing, but there was something missing that she was not finding in the Catholic Church. As hard as it was to try something so radically different, going to the Waters turned out to be a blessing.

"You always feel so much better when you leave," Wendy said. "We're very happy there. It's not where I would have seen myself ten years ago, but it's where we need to be right now."

Wendy still does not have answers for why Brian was killed that night, but she feels his presence, and she believes that he knows what's going on. He's still watching over her and Katelyn, and now the rest of her family as well.

She believes she will see him again, and then maybe she will have her questions answered.

"I always say that when I get there I'm going to ask some of those," she said. "But I'm hoping I won't care at that point."

For now Wendy said she has moved on from asking, "Why me?" to asking, "Why not me?" She's moved to acknowledging that tragedy happens, and as much as it's not something you ask for or want, you must deal with it.

She has done that. The Klinefelters have done that. For now, that's enough.

"I feel like we not only survived it, but we thrived," Wendy said. "I'm so grateful for that. I know people who go through hard times and end up being broken by it and never recovering. That would be an even greater tragedy."

Acknowledgements

This book would not have been possible if many people had not been willing to open up about their personal emotional experiences. Special thanks must go to Doug Thomsen, who was the first to trust me with his story and got the ball rolling.

The list of people who sat down with me after that, either in person or over the phone, is long: Ruth Tamm, Tiffany Breth, Mary Christen Czech, Roger Anhorn, Stewart Wirth, Brad Lindgren, Gerald Staehling, Jon Anderson, Marv Siekman, Luke Ahlschlager, Matthew Shirkey, Scott Warzecha and Valerie Silva.

Thanks also go to the Stearns County Attorney's Office for pulling all the court files that helped fill the gaps.

Special thanks must go to the Klinefelters: Sarah, Jason, Greg, Lois, Dave, and the Tragiais: Wendy, Katelyn and John. It was an honor to meet you all.

About the Author

Andy Marso grew up in St. Cloud and graduated from Cathedral High School before leaving Minnesota to attend the University of Kansas. He has written for the *St. Cloud Times*, *Washington Post* and *Topeka Capital-Journal*, among other publications. He lives in Topeka, where he is a journalist for the Kansas Health Institute News Service. His first book, *Worth the Pain: How Meningitis Nearly Killed Me—Then Changed My Life for the Better*, is available on Amazon.